THE TAO-TEH-KING

SAYINGS OF LAO-TZU

One of the greatest sages of history was a man named Lao-tzu, who was born in China in the year 604 B.C. He is regarded as the founder of the system of religion known as Taoism. His writings have been preserved in a small volume of poetry entitled *Tao-Teh-King*, which translated means "The Way and Its Power," or "The Book of the Way and Its Virtue." It has also been called "A Scripture of the Eternal and Its Characteristics," and it was adopted as a canon in the year 666 A.D. during the rule of the Emperor Kao Tsung of the T'ang Dynasty. Because of its sublime and timeless concepts, the *Tao-Teh-King* has endured through the centuries; it has been translated into many languages, and has been the subject of numerous volumes of philosophical and speculative literature.

This version of the *Tao-Teh-King* was first published in 1905. The translator, C. Spurgeon Medhurst, went to China as a missionary and during his twenty years in that country came to regard Lao-tzu's work as a spiritual and inspirational guide. A scholar of the Chinese language, he did a great deal of research and consulted the works of other scholars, in both English and Chinese, before completing his own effort. Being at the same time a student of comparative religion and metaphysics, he added his own interesting commentary and notes, comparing many of the sayings with similar concepts in other scriptures and teachings.

Because of the interest in Chinese culture, and the enduring value of Lao-tzu's message, this book is now made available as part of the Quest Book series.

THE
TAO-TEH-KING
SAYINGS OF LAO-TZU

translated with commentary by

C. SPURGEON MEDHURST

THE THEOSOPHICAL PUBLISHING HOUSE
Wheaton, Ill., U.S.A.
Madras, India / London, England

© Copyright The Theosophical Publishing House 1972

The Theosophical Publishing House is a department of The Theosophical Society in America, Wheaton, Illinois

Original edition 1905

Revised Quest Book edition 1972

Library of Congress Catalog Card Number: 72-83648

ISBN: 0-8356-0430-6

Manufactured in the United States of America

PUBLISHER'S NOTE

In preparing this edition for publication, some editorial revisions have been made in the commentary and notes, mainly to update the printing style and to omit some passages which are no longer relevant. No change has been made in the actual translation of *The Tao-Teh-King*, which remains as given by the translator.

FOREWORD

"In every nation he that feareth him, and worketh righteousness, is acceptable to him." The Spirit of God is confined to no sect, religion, race or creed. Wherever hearts are still and aspirations pure the vision may dawn, the voice of inspiration be heard. God has spoken to man in many languages, and the translator of the present work was supported throughout what was often an arduous task by the belief that the *Tao-teh-king* is a message from the Divine. Like all ancient writings, it may have suffered at the hands of time, but as I have endeavored to show in my notes and comments on the text, the teaching is one which the inner consciousness of all ages has recognized as THE TRUTH. Though Lao-tzu's accent is his own, it is easily seen to be but a dialect of the universal tongue. "And I say unto you, that many shall come from the east and the west, and shall recline with Abraham, and Isaac, and Jacob, in the kingdom of heaven."

There are many editions of the *Tao-teh-king*, but has Lao-tzu ever really been translated? If I have succeeded in any measure it is because I have built on the labors of others. The Chinese is difficult, and mistakes are perhaps inevitable, but I have consulted in detail the works of Legge, Balfour, Giles, Carus, Kingsmill, Maclagan, Old and von Strauss. Although unable to agree with any of these in their interpretations, to all I am indebted for guidance and suggestions while working my way through the terse obscurity of the Chinese.

7

In the course of my researches I have consulted nearly an equal number of Chinese commentaries. I confess that long before I dreamed of being presumptuous enough to endeavor to translate Lao-tzu I was accustomed to carrying his writing with me as a sort of spiritual *vade mecum*. My present rendering of the ancient philosopher is not so much a specimen of scholarship as the humble offering of a disciple.

The difficulties which lie across the pathway of anyone attempting such a work may be illustrated by a quotation from Dr. Legge's preface to the *Yi King* (Sacred Books of the East), vol. 16: "The written characters of the Chinese," writes this eminent scholar, "are not representations of words, but symbols of ideas, . . . the combination of them in composition is not a representation of what the writer would say, but of what he thinks. It is vain, therefore, for a translator to attempt a literal version. . . . In the study of a Chinese classical book there is not so much an interpretation of the characters employed by the writer as a participation of his thoughts—there is a seeing of mind to mind." In this last sentence the Doctor has unconsciously explained why he so signally failed in his efforts to render Lao-tzu into English. Prof. Legge, one of the foremost Chinese scholars of his day, was wholly Confucianist in his sympathies, and it is a pity that so faulty a translation as is his version of the *Tao-teh-king* should have obtained the prominence and importance which it derives from its inclusion in "The Sacred Books of the East."

It only remains for me to add that I have made no attempt to accomplish the impossible and reproduce the measured rhythm of the original, but have contented myself with rendering the whole into as clear and concise English as possible, without reference to the regulated cadences in which a large part of the Chinese has been written.

In his *Remains of Lao-tzu,* Prof. Giles has endeavored

8

to prove that there is very little of the real Lao-tzu in the essay which goes under his name. Though perhaps few scholars would follow Mr. Giles in all his slashing criticisms, it may be admitted that the shadowy and broken progression in the development of the basic ideas of the *Tao-teh-king,* together with the seemingly needless repetitions, suggest that what we have are but the higher peaks of a submerged continent, not the entire map of the old mystic's scheme. The thought of the book is a buried thought, the connections of its sentences spiritual rather than grammatical. Divided into two parts, part I may be described as "metaphysical," part II as "moral," but the division is rough and not accurate. If such a liberty were taken, it would be comparatively easy to rearrange the sections into a more orderly sequence than now.

Confucianism and Taoism

In dealing with the *Tao-teh-king,* it is hardly possible to avoid some reference to the sister religion, Confucianism, since it sprang from the same soil and from among the same people. Both Lao-tzu and Confucius appeal to pre-existing authorities. Before their day the two systems probably formed one ideal plan for life; since then, however, there has been a growing tendency to separate the practical ethics of the one from the metaphysical mysticism of the other. Yet many devout Confucianists study Lao-tzu's classic with deep interest.

Lao-tzu, like Buddha, would extirpate desire; Confucius, like the Stoics, would ignore it. The asceticism of Lao-tzu is matched by the self-sufficiency of Confucius, and each agrees that the desire which ends in self is an evil. As regards cosmogony, it is interesting to note that while the practical Confucianist has a metaphysical explanation for the origin of the universe, the metaphysical Lao-tzu is content to put forward his Tao as an explanation of the whole, without attempting to say *how* anything came to be.

9

Tao

Lao-tzu's Tao, which is as untranslatable as the algebraic x, and which von Strauss, in the thirty-third section of his introduction to the *Tao-teh-king*, compares to the Sanskrit *buddhi*, has much in common with the Primeval Fire or Aether of Heraclitus. The properties of mind and matter may be attributed to both; both become transformed into the elements; and in both the elements vanish into the primordial All, though Lao-tzu, of course, gives us nothing like the theologic-cosmogonical system of the Greek.

Lao-tzu presents us with the Tao under two aspects—the undifferentiated Nameless, and the differentiated Universal Life. In this he agrees with the *Bhagavad Gita* of Hinduism, in which we read: "There are two Purushas in this world, the destructible and the indestructible; the destructible (is) all beings, the unchanging (is) called the indestructible." (15-16.) Again as in the Confucian cosmogony, The Absolute or The Unlimited is always behind The Great Extreme from whose vibrations everything sprang; so there lies behind the Tao, which is nameable, the Tao which cannot be named.

The Sages

Notwithstanding Lao-tzu's reverence for the mysterious, he never sacrifices Man to the Divine. On the contrary, throughout the *Tao-teh-king*, the individuality of the True Man is emphasized in every possible way. The goal of humanity is only possible by complete union with the Tao—the Ultimate Unity of the Universe. If the *Tao-teh-king* teaches anything it certainly teaches this. Thus, like all religions in all ages, Lao-tzu points to yoga or union, as the *summum bonum* of existence. The perfected men, or the sages, are those who have attained to this great good. "As the branch cannot bear fruit of itself except it abide in the vine, so neither can ye, except ye abide in me. I am the vine, ye are the branches."

Government

The weakest part of Lao-tzu's teachings may perhaps be thought to be his utopian conceptions of a model state. Like Plato, he seems to have thought that "until kings are philosophers, or philosophers are kings, cities will never cease from ill," and not only like Plato does he appear to consider the study of economics, law, or finance as unnecessary qualifications for a legislator, but he requires no education for the citizens of his ideal republic. Spirituality rather than political economy is to be the basis of this strange kingdom. Its appeals are not made to men's hopes and fears, but to the calm passionlessness of their higher natures. Its controlling force is not militarism, but spiritual culture. Both rulers and people obtain all they require by the abstract contemplation of an abstract good. Everything is reduced to the purest simplicity. In many respects Lao-tzu's completed society corresponds to the "natural and spiritual theocracy" which Saint Martin of Tours describes in his *Lettre a un ami sur La Revolution Francaise*.

Lao-tzu loves paradox, and his sayings are frequently as paradoxical as the sayings in the Gospels. In his extreme assertions as to what constitutes a perfect state he is endeavoring to show that righteousness alone exalteth a nation, and that whatever clouds the nation's conceptions of *this* is worse than valueless. The student must never forget that Lao-tzu, being a mystic, is no more susceptible to literal interpretation when he deals with the concrete than are the words of Jesus, "Cast not your pearls before swine." No absolute rule of conduct is conveyed by this expression, yet who does not perfectly understand its meaning? So with Lao-tzu's politics; they are physical illustrations of spiritual truths. Lao-tzu's only concern is that the government

11

shall give free development to the individual spiritual life of each citizen in the state; this secured, an autocracy might equal a democracy. A passage in Epictetus illustrates Lao-tzu's position: "Do this, do not this, or I will cast thee into prison—this is not a rule for reasoning beings. But—'As Zeus has ordered so do thou act; but if thou dost not thou shalt suffer loss and hurt.' What hurt? None other than this—not to have done what it behooved thee to do. Thou shalt lose faith, piety, decency—look for no greater injury than these." So Lao-tzu reduces life to the utmost simplicity, that nothing may interfere with the contemplation of the Tao. The never absent presence of this perfect ideal in the mind will be enough to keep the people from trespassing either in thought, speech or action. Such an accomplishment is better than all that the finest civilizations offer.

Here again we may observe the difference between Lao-tzu and his contemporary, Confucius. Both were politicians, but while Confucius would regulate the state by extra rules of conduct, multiplied until they covered every department of life, Lao-tzu sought the same end by the purification of the inner being. Little wonder that when Confucius, whose field of vision was almost entirely objective, visited Lao-tzu, who was almost as much concerned with the subjective, he returned bewildered, and said to his disciples (I quote Dr. Carus's translation of the Chinese historian's record) : "I know that the birds can fly; I know that the fishes can swim; I know that the wild animals can run. For the running, one could make nooses; for the swimming, one could make nets; for the flying, one could make arrows. As to the dragon, I cannot know how he can bestride wind and clouds when he heavenwards rises. Today I saw Lao-Tze. Is he perhaps like the dragon?" Others, like Confucius, may be inclined to ask the same question, but "he that hath ears to hear, let him hear."

Ethics

It must not, however, be supposed that Lao-tzu's system is non-ethical and impractical. On the contrary, in his doctrine of non-attachment, or non-action, the old mystic supplies us with the very essence of all morality. He holds that nature provides a perfect example in her inactive activity. The vegetable kingdom is Lao-tzu's ideal. In the cultivated garden everything is in order, everything is separate. It is not this, however, which so much interests Lao-tzu as the quiet detachment of vegetable life. It plants without seeking the fruit; it never mars by its effort to accomplish; everything is left to develop according to its own nature. Here Lao-tzu has an echo in Emerson, who in his essay on "Spiritual Laws," writes: "Action and inaction are alike. One piece of the tree is cut for the weathercock, and one for the sleeper of a bridge; the virtue of the wood is apparent in both." Well will it be for this restless, weary, discontented age if it comprehend this message of action in non-action and non-action in action which comes to it out of the dim past, from the great Loess Plains of Northwest China.

Said one greater than Lao-tzu: "So is the kingdom of God, as if a man should cast seed upon the earth; and should sleep and rise night and day, and the seed should spring up and grow, he knoweth not how." "The kingdom of heaven is like unto a grain of mustard seed, which a man took and sowed in his field; which indeed is less than all seeds; but when it is grown it is greater than the herbs, and becometh a tree, so that the birds of the heaven come and lodge in the branches thereof." "The kingdom of heaven is like unto leaven, which a woman took and hid in three measures of meal, till it was all leavened." There is a striking similarity between these sayings of Jesus and the teaching of the *Tao-teh-king*. Lao-tzu's doctrine of non-attachment, or non-action, found its loftiest expression on the cross on Calvary.

13

Summary

This, then, is the word which this ancient writing has for the world—a life of sensation is a life of instability, a life of non-accomplishment. Until the "final facts of consciousness" are understood, true peace is impossible, but when these are known, detachment from action for the sake of action will be the result. "If any man love the world (is attached to the sensuous) the love of the Father is not in him." So says the Christian mystic, John. He who has not attained to non-attachment or non-action is a stranger to the power of the Tao; this is the cry of the Chinese mystic, Lao-tzu.

Victor von Strauss summarizes Lao-tzu's teaching thus: "Man's moral worth consists of what he has, not of what he does; it has respect not only to what he is in himself, but to his influence on others. It is what a man is which makes his acts good, and not the deeds which make the man. The higher the moral worth of the man the less he values his own acts, and the less likely is he to seek justification through his works. In this way he influences his fellows, not so much through what he does as through what he is; not so much through his speech as through his conduct." (*Wandel*) "But to him that worketh not, but believeth on him that justifieth the ungodly, his faith is reckoned for righteousness." Confucius represents the James, Lao-tzu the Paul, of Christian theology.

INTRODUCTION

Carlyle somewhere compares religion to an "everlasting lode-star, that beams the brighter in the heavens the darker here on earth grows the night around him," and it is doubtful whether but for the degeneracy of his time we should ever have received this most precious fragment from antiquity, known as the *Tao-teh-king*. Lao-tzu,* alias Lao-chün, alias Lao-tan (born 604 B.C.), was one of those God-instructed souls who, having mastered "the fortuitous in life," stepped out from the shadow of the temporal into the clear, serene atmosphere of the Divine.

A keeper of the records in the capital of the state of Chou, he retired from office because he saw how corrupt society had become, rendering all real spirituality impossible. Rather than become tainted by what he felt unable to change, he put aside earthly ambition and retired from the world. The historian says of him: "No one knows where he died." Before leaving the haunts of men, however, he wrote the *Tao-teh-king,* at the request of his friend, the custom house officer at the frontier. This man's name was Yin-hsi, a name which deserves to be recorded.

I have already referred to Confucius's opinion of his famous contemporary. There is no proof that they met more than once, the interviews between the two which embellish the works of Chuang-tzu, Lao-tzu's chief disciple, being the inventions of the active brain of that clever writer, and intended to bring the system of Confucianism into ridicule. It is the beginning of a breach

---

* Often spelled Lao Tsze.

which should never have been made.

The *Tao-teh-king,* or, "A Scripture of the Eternal and Its Characteristics," was first adopted as a canon 666 A.D., at which date the Emperor Kao Tsung of the T'ang dynasty gave Lao-tzu the posthumous title, "The Supreme Monarch of the Profoundest Mystery." Later rulers added to his honors, and legend relates wonderful tales concerning him. His mother is said to have given birth to him 1321 B.C., bringing him forth from her left side as she sat under a plum tree (the name of the family was Li, or Plum). He is said to have been then an old man, having remained for eighty years in his mother's womb. Hence his designation, Lao-tzu, or "Old Boy." By others he is called Lao-chün, or "Ancient Sire," or Lao-tan, "the venerable Long Lobed," big lobes being considered a mark of virtue. Later Taoist writings have been ascribed to him, the compositions commencing "The Most Supreme Master saith," or "The Supreme One saith," but there is no proof that Lao-tzu wrote anything besides the *Tao-teh-king.* The other scriptures of the same school all bear its impress written largely across their pages.

In the "Trinity of Tranquillity" of modern Taoism, which bears no more relation to the Taoism of Lao-tzu than do the rigid institutes of Calvin to the teachings of Jesus as recorded in the Gospels, Lao-tzu occupies the first place. Modern Taoism is a system of alchemy and polytheism which regards the soul and the body as identical in substance, and maintains that by physical discipline their dissolution may be prevented. Lao-tzu, indeed, hinted at the possibility of obtaining an ascendancy over matter, and to such hints in the *Tao-teh-king,* and to the Confucian *Yi-king,* the science of alchemy, which may be described as the germ of the modern evolutionary theory, probably owes its birth. Born in China, alchemy traveled to Europe via Arabia. The vocabularies of the older Eastern and the later Western schools are in many instances similar, and the ends and methods of both appear the same. Lao-tzu, however, was no alchemist, and for this he is satirized by the famous Chinese poet, Pei-chu-yi (772-846 A.D.). He is ever speaking of the Tao and its energies, says the poet; throughout his five thousand words (the *Tao-teh-king* contains 5,320 characters) he says nothing of transmutations or genii, but only talks about reaching heaven. The old mystic was indeed incapable of conceiving anything but the purest spirituality, whereas his more materialistic successors have made his slight hints at the powers of occultism the foundations of a scheme for mastering the protean powers of transmutation, which, whatever may be said of their European confrères, would, as far as it is possible to form an opinion, seem to have objects which can only be described as selfish.

The other two members of the Trinity of which Lao-tzu is now the chief are the mythical P'an-ku, the First Being brought into existence by cosmogonical evolution, whose breath became the wind; whose voice is the thunder; whose left eye is the sun; whose right eye is the moon, etc.; and Yü Huang Shang-ti, a magician named Chang, who raced another magician, named Lu, up to heaven. Both rode dragons, and Chang won. Some Western scholars think that Lao-tzu also is a myth, a mere creation of the imagination. The materials for an exhaustive examination of the matter are not at hand, but no Chinese has ever doubted that the *Tao-teh-king* was the genuine production of a genuine sage named Lao-tan or Lao-tzu, and written just before he left China forever, through the Han-ku Pass.

It may be added that the *Tao-teh-king* is the only Taoist book which the Chinese Buddhists esteem. They relate a legend to the effect that one of the Buddhist emperors of China, in order to test the relative divinity of the two religions, ordered each sect to pile their books on an altar and burn them. The Buddhist scriptures would not burn, but the Taoist writings quickly flamed up at the application of the torch. Much alarmed, the Taoist priests in attendance tried to snatch their precious manuscripts from the fire, but they only pulled out one, the *Tao-teh-king*.

At about the time when Lao-tzu lived a wave of spiritual enlightenment appears to have swept over the world. Especially in Asia was there a general movement towards higher and clearer thought. In India and in Persia, as well as in China, religious revolutions were in progress. The exact date of Lao's birth, like most of the facts of his life, is shrouded in obscurity, but most opinion is that he was born during the early part of the sixth century before Christ. Confucius was born 550 B.C., Pythagoras forty or fifty years earlier. Thales, the first of the seven wise men of Greece, was born in 639 or 636 B.C., and two or three years later, Solon. The reformation in Iran, or ancient Persia, connected with the name of Zoroaster or Zerduscht, was probably contemporaneous. The Buddha arose in India a little later, and the Hebrew prophets of the captivity enriched the same age.

This brief introduction, which might easily have been expanded into a volume, may well be closed with a few appreciations of Lao-tzu from some of the many Oriental scholars who have studied his pages.

Victor von Strauss says of Lao-tzu's work that it contains "a grasp of thought, a height of contemplation, a purity of conception in the things of God, such as we seek in vain anywhere in pre-Christian time, except in the Jewish Scriptures."

Says Paul Carus: "Lao Tsze was one of the greatest men that ever trod our earth." "One of the most remarkable thinkers of mankind." "The *Tao-teh-king* is an indispensable book, and no one who is interested in religion can afford to leave it unread."

"The plan of the *Tao-teh-king*," says J. Edkins, "is to begin with the absolute and to unfold in obscure language, so as to do something to teach in broad outlines and with a few touches the mystery of the universe." "He is, the greatest of Chinese philosophers." (Vide *Ancient Symbolism,* by J. Edkins.)

Rev. John Chalmers, shows in his introduction to his translation of Lao-tzu's work that the philosopher "penetrated about as deeply into the mystery of the universe as the famous German metaphysician Schelling," while M. Abel-Remusàt contends that the doctrines commonly attributed to Pythagoras, Plato, and their disciples, are to be found in Lao-tzu.

Georg von der Gabelentz, of Leipzig, describes the *Tao-teh-king* as "one of the most eminent masterpieces of Chinese literature, one of the profoundest philosophical books the world has ever produced, and one the authenticity of which has been least contested in his fatherland and even in the circle of European sinologues."

Samuel Johnson, in his *Oriental Religions* writes of the *Tao-teh-king*: "It is a book of wonderful ethical and spiritual simplicity, and deals neither in speculative cosmogony nor in popular superstitions. . . . It is in practical earnest, and speaks from the heart and to the heart. Its religion resembles that of Fenelon or Thomas à Kempis, combined with a perceptive rationality of which they were not masters."

The eminent scholar, James Legge states: "The Taoism of the present day is a system of the wildest polytheism. . . . He ought not to bear the obloquy of being the founder of the Taoist religion."

As Mr. Ball says in *Things Chinese*: "In this Laotzu, the founder of Taoism, we have one of those men whose writings, life, and reputed actions have exerted an untold influence on the course of human life in this world, but of whom the world, during his lifetime, took so little account that all that is authentically known about him may be summed up in a few lines."

May this effort to increase the range of the Old Chinese mystic's influence communicate to others some of the quiet peace which the study of his work has brought to the translator.

C. SPURGEON MEDHURST

Let not him that seeketh cease from his search until he find, and when he finds he shall wonder; wondering he shall reach the kingdom, and when he reaches the kingdom he shall have rest.—*A Logion of Jesus.*

Read not to contradict and refute, nor to believe and take for granted, nor to find talk and discourse, but to weigh and consider.—*Lord Bacon.*

CHAPTER 1

The Tao which can be expressed is not the unchanging Tao;[1] the name which can be named is not the unchanging name.

The nameless is the beginning of the Heaven Earth;[2] the mother of all things[3] is the nameable.

Thus, while the eternal not-being[4] leads toward the fathomless, the eternal being conducts to the boundary. Although these two[5] have been differently named they come from the same.[6]

As the same they may be described as the abysmal. The abyss of the abysmal[7] is the gate of all mystery.

Comment

That aspect of God which is hidden in eternity, without bounds, without limits, without beginning, must be distinguished from that side of God which is expressed in nature and in man. The one, apparently subjective, certainly unknowable; the other, a self-manifestation, or a going forth, the commencement of our knowledge, as of our being. "No man hath seen God at any time, the only begotten Son, which is in the bosom of the Father, He hath declared Him." Whether "the only begotten Son" be identified with an historical person or not, the conception is necessary to any thought of God. Without a self-revelation, the Eternal Presence remains unknown. Hence the Indian has his avataras, the Christian his incarnation.

Lao-tzu is strictly logical when he ascribes the origin of all phenomena to the manifesting Deity, rather than to the Undifferentiated One, which being changeless *could* not create.

Says Herbert Spencer: "The antithesis of subject and object, never to be transcended while consciousness lasts, renders impossible all knowledge of the Ultimate Reality in which subject and object are united." (*Principles of Psychology*, vol. 1, 272.)

Notes

(1) Hsü-hui-hi sagely observes that as names always leave the essence unnamed it is certain that no name can express the Tao.

(2) The noumenal or *arupa* world—the world of causes.

(3) The phenomenal or *rupa* world—the world of effects.

(4) Yet, as Hsü-hui-hi says, the very term "Not-Being" is misleading, for the Tao is absolutely inexpressible.

(5) The Tao in its twofold aspect.

(6) i. e. That which is above Being and Not-Being.

(7) Whence both Being and Not-Being emerge.

Seek not for a name for God; for you will not find any: For everything that is named is named by its letter so that the latter gives the name and the former gives ear. Who then is he who hath given God a name? "God" is not a "name," but an "opinion about God."—*Sextus.*

"There was when naught was; nay even that 'naught' was not aught of things that are. . . . For that 'naught' is not simply the so-called ineffable; it is beyond that. For that which is *really* ineffable is not named ineffable, but is superior to every name that is used."—*Basilides.* (vide *Fragments of a Faith Forgotten* by G. R. S. Mead.)

CHAPTER 2

When everyone in the world became conscious of the beauty of the beautiful it turned to evil; they became conscious of the goodness of the good and ceased to be good.[1] Thus not-being and being arise the one from the other. So also do the difficult and the easy; the long and the short; the high and the low; sounds and voices; the preceding and the following.

Therefore[2] the Holy Man abides by non-attachment in his affairs, and practices a doctrine which cannot be imparted by speech. He attends to everything in its turn and declines nothing; produces without claiming; acts without dwelling thereon; completes his purposes without resting in them. Inasmuch as he does this he loses nothing.[3]

Comment

A lotus pond will serve as an illustration of the difference between the holy sages and the younger members of the race. Covered with broad green leaves and brilliant blooms, it irresistibly attracts child-souls. They wade into the water, sink in the slime, and desperately struggle for the fragile petals; but the sages, their elder brethren, remain quietly on the bank, always alert to aid any who require assistance, content to admire, content to enjoy, without desiring to possess; yet actually owning the flowers more truly than the struggling crowd in the slimy pond. We are feeblest when we are grasping.

"The Master said, 'Those who are without virtue, cannot abide long either in a condition of poverty and hardship, or in a condition of enjoyment.' "—*Analects of Confucius.*

"To dwell in the wide house of the world, to stand in the correct seat of the world, and to walk in the great path of

23

the world; when he obtains his desire for office, to practice his principles for the good of the people; and when that desire is disappointed, to practice them alone; to be above the power of riches and honors to make dissipated, of poverty and mean condition to make swerve from principle, and of power and force to make bend—these characteristics constitute the great man."—Mencius.

Notes

(1) Cf. chap. 18.

(2) Because the antimonies in the text are in the outer world of consciousness only, having no existence in the inner world of spirit, the sage makes no distinction. All things are alike to him (cf. chap. 63). Says the *Bhagavad-Gita*—"Thy business is with action only, never with its fruits; so let not the fruit of thy action be thy motive, nor be thou to inaction attached."

(3) "A pure, single, and stable spirit is not distracted though it be employed in many works; for that it doeth all to the honor of God, and being at rest within, seeketh not itself in anything it doth."—*Of the Imitation of Christ*, bk. 1, ch. 3.

"Balanced in pleasure and pain, self-reliant, to whom a lump of earth, a rock and gold are alike; the same to loved and unloved, firm, the same in censure and in praise, the same in honor and ignominy, the same to friend and foe, abandoning all undertakings—he is said to have crossed over the Gunas." *Bhagavad-Gita*—14: 24, 25.

CHAPTER 3

When worth is not honored the people may be kept from strife.

When rare articles are not valued the people are kept from theft.

When the desirable is left unnoticed the heart is not confused.

Therefore, the method of government by the Holy Man is to empty the heart, while strengthening the purpose; to make the will pliant, and the character strong.[1] He ever keeps the people simple-minded and passionless, so that the world-wise do not dare to plan.

Practice non-action and everything will be regulated.[2]

Comment

Jesus, the chief of transcendentalists, summed up the law of life in the command to love God with the whole being, and demanded of his disciples that they bless their enemies, and cherish the same feelings toward their neighbors as they felt for themselves. They were to have no treasures on earth, nor were they to occupy their thoughts with providing for the physical—an ideal which will only be reached as men rise higher than the sense life of hearing, seeing, smelling, tasting, feeling. All outer goods are forgotten when man's inner being is filled with the luster of God. So long as the driving force of man's life is desire, so long will he fall short of the teachings of the Savior. When, however, he rises above the bondage of the senses, when he perceives the human soul in all its glory, as the temple of the Holy God, his motives will be as the motives of the Godhead, the standard set up by Christ will be attained. Neither rewards nor punishments will longer appeal to him. The subtle selfishness which the one addresses, and the base fear which the other influences, will alike be alien to his character.

In this ideal republic, the commonwealth of days to come, socialism will realize its noblest ambitions. Each will help his brother forward, and find his joy in seeing the prosperity of his neighbor. Theft will be unheard of, for "rare articles" will be no more prized. The very fact that they are rare, and therefore not within the reach of all, will deprive them of their worth.

How it will be possible for this to become *un fait accompli* we may perhaps realize by reference to the law of vibrations. As the vibrations which produce the phenomenon of telepathy would, if completely under control, make man independent of the lower vibrations which make speech possible, so when the higher vibrations of the spiritual alone vibrate, the lower vibrations of the earthly will be sought no more. The pure spiritualism of Jesus will be universal among men. They will see God. By ceasing from desire, everything that is desirable will be obtained. Desire stifles; only the desireless breathe God's atmosphere. "Christian prayer itself is a moderation of desire. It is a refusal any longer to say of everything, 'It is mine.' It is the refusal to ask that which will lift me above other people. It is the cry to have my garments parted among the multitude."

Notes

(1) Lit.—"To make their minds vacant, their stomachs comfortable, their wills weak, and their bones strong." Cf. Isa. lviii. 11.

(2) Cp. chaps. 63, 65.

CHAPTER 4

The Tao is as emptiness, so are its operations. It resembles non-fullness.[1]

Fathomless! It seems to be the ancestor of all form.

It removes sharpness, unravels confusion, harmonizes brightness, and becomes one with everything.

Pellucid![2] It bears the appearance of permanence.

I know not whose son it is. Its Noumenon (εἰδωλον) was before the Lord.[3]

Comment

No matter what road we take, we find "No thoroughfare" conspicuously displayed at the end. Hence Lao-tzu describes his never absent Presence, intangible yet omnipresent, formless yet the Father of form, as *"Emptiness"*—apprehensible but not comprehensible. The thought of man can only proceed in certain limited directions, and therefore This, the Ubiquitous, "containing everything, yet contained in all," cannot be explained. Whoever would perceive It must leave the beaten track of routine, and in a solitary by-way go forward by the single aid of the higher intuitive powers. Furthermore, It, the one comprehensive Unit, *"resembles non-fulness,"* for we only know the perceptions It excites in our consciousness, never adequate to represent that which is the Consciousness of all consciousness.

Notes

(1) He who understands it desires nothing. "What is kingdom to us, O Govinda, what enjoyment or even life?"— *Bhagavad-Gita* (The Despondency of Arjuna).

(2) Rev. iv, 6. Undefiled by contact.

(3) "God was not the Lord—in the creature only hath he become the Lord, I ask to be rid of the Lord; that is, that the Lord by his grace would bring me into the Essence,

which is before the Lord, and above distinction. I would enter into that Eternal Unity which was mine before all time, above all addition and diminution—into that immobility whereby all is moved."—Meister Eckhart.

"Eternity is unborn and eternal. God is born into the Godhead when he begins to create. The Creator creates himself. He is the Creator because he calls the creation into being. The word rests in God until it begins to be uttered, even as the thought rests in man until it has been conceived."—Dr. Franz Hartmann.

"There are two forms of Brahman, time and non-time. That which was before the sun is non-time and has no parts. That which had its beginning from the sun is time and has parts."

"Two Brahmans have to be meditated on, the word and the non-word. By the word alone is the non-word revealed."

"Two Brahmans are to be known, the word-Brahman and the highest Brahman; he who is perfect in the word-Brahman attains the highest Brahman."—Upanishads. (Sacred Books of the East, vol. 15, pp. 317 and 321.)

"Perfect personality is to be found only in God, while in all finite spirits there exists only a weak imitation of personality; the finiteness of the finite is not a productive condition of personality, but rather a limiting barrier to its perfect development."—Lao-tzu.

CHAPTER 5

Nature is non-benevolent. It regards all things as straw dogs.[1]

The Holy Man is non-benevolent.[2] He regards the masses as straw dogs.

The space between the heaven and the earth is like a bellows; though unsupported, it does not warp; when in motion the more it expels.[3]

Though words could exhaust this theme, they would not be so profitable as the preservation of its inner essence.[4]

Comment

Nature cares as little for the divisions among men as the ancient Chinese worshipers for the straw dogs which had served their sacrificial functions. The law of cause and effect, order and sequence (karma), is as exact, universal and scientific in the realm of mind and spirit as in the domain of physics and mathematics. Every language bears in its proverbs deep traces of its workings. Solomon's adage, "He that soweth iniquity shall reap calamity . . . he that hath a bountiful eye shall be blessed," has its counterpart in the sayings of all peoples. Say the Chinese, "Sow beans and you will reap beans; plant melons and you will reap melons. One cannot plant bitter gourds and reap sweet tasting fruit." "Heaven is bountiful to all according to their deserts; on the good it showers felicities, on the not good it inflicts calamity." But though man may not escape the law, man can deprive it of evil by his attitude toward its results. Hence worshipful humility is more fitting than argument. "Stand in awe and sin not: commune with your own heart upon your bed and be still." "The Lord is in his holy temple: be silent before him all the earth." The solemn mysteries of life are not to be profaned.

Notes

(1) "Before the grass-dogs are set forth (at the sacrifice) they are deposited in a box or basket and wrapped up with

elegantly embroidered cloths, while the representative of the dead and the officer of prayer prepare themselves by fasting to present them. After they have been set forth, however, passersby trample on their heads and backs, and the grass-cutters take and burn them in cooking. This is all they are good for." Chuang Tzu.

Says the *Yin-fu-king*: "Heaven's greatest mercy is that it is without mercy." See I. Pet. 1, 17. Cp. *Tao-teh-king*, ch. 49.

(2) Compare A. P. Sinnett's description of the Adept or Mahatma: "He has attained that love of humanity as a whole which transcends the love of the Maya or illusion;" i. e., he regards all with equal impartiality.—*Esoteric Buddhism*.

(3) The Chinese explanation is that the seasons follow each other with unvarying regularity, ever pouring forth new forms of life from its bellows like a mouth providing the wicked and the good alike with all that they require. Cp. Matt. v. 45.

The esotericist will probably be reminded here of Bhuvarloka. See *The Secret Doctrine*, by H. P. Blavatsky, vol. 3, p. 568, et seq.

(4) "To thee silence is praise, O God."—Delitzsch's translation of Psalm lxv. 1.

CHAPTER 6

The Valley-God never dies. She may be styled the Mother of the Abyss. The Abysmal Mother's orifice may be called the Root of the Heaven-Earth.

Continuous she is as though ever abiding, and may be employed without weariness.[1]

Comment

The word *ku,* here and elsewhere translated "valley," is one of Lao-tzu's difficult key-words. Authorities agree that the word as used in the *Tao-teh-king* does not refer to the visible vale in which vegetation grows, but to the empty (?) space enclosed by the hills—a characteristic example of our author's fine power of compression.

It is significant that Lao-tzu's concept of space is never an endless extension without limitation, but always something that is bounded—the space confined between two hills, a valley. Two ideas are here suggested: 1. That cosmic-space is a portion only of the illimitable field, marked off or set apart by the Eternal, within which his activities operate. This is bounded by two eternities—a manvantara between pralayas. 2. That creation is a valley, a self-limitation or humiliation of the All-Consciousness.

Hence in the text the "Valley-God" (or Spirit, the original is incapable of exact definition) corresponds to Aditi, "The Boundless" (Akasha), otherwise known as the Deva Matri or the Mother of the Gods (Cosmic Space). We have still another aspect of her in the *Rig-veda,* where she is described as Vach, "Mystic Speech"—the root whence occult wisdom proceeds. We meet her again in the teaching of the Kabalists as the female Logos, or Sephira, the mother of the Sephiroth. In the Old Testament we find her personified as Wisdom, the Chokmah, or male Sephira of *the Zohar,* for, as Philo points out, THIS is both male and female—perfect wholeness.

The commentator Su-cheh says: "The epithet 'valley' here applied to God (or spirit) expresses existence in the midst of non-existence, and as THAT is unborn, it is undying. It is called God (or spirit) to express its perfections, and 'Mother of the Abyss' because of its achievements. All Nature springs from the Mother, who is called abysmal, because, while we can perceive what She produces, her methods of production remain inscrutable."

The word *ku* recurs in chaps. 15, 28, 32, 39, 41 and 66, but not again in this connection.

Notes

(1) Dr. Edkins interprets this passage as referring to "the ultimate principle of nature," which is without definite form or feature."—*China Review*, vol. 13, p. 11.

See Frederic Henry Balfour's translation of the "*T'ai-Hsi' King*, or The Respiration of the Embryo." *China Review*, vol. 9, p. 224.

CHAPTER 7

Nature[1] continues long. What is the reason that Nature continues long? Because it produces nothing for itself it is able to constantly produce.

It is for this reason that the Holy Man puts himself in the background; yet he comes to the front. He is indifferent to himself; yet he is preserved.

Is it not because he has no interests of his own that he is able to secure his interests?

Comment

The myth of Psyche and Eros is an exquisite illustration of the tragedy and mystery of life. Through seeking to gratify selfish curiosity Psyche lost all she cared for, and not until she had been purified by unmeasured suffering did she meet her beloved again. The Prodigal in Christ's parable only found his father when he lost all desire for a separated will.

Those who seek least enjoy most. Lao-tzu's allegory is one with the paradox of Jesus, that life is best found when lost, and most lost when found, for only the all-loving know life, and only the disinterested love all.

Note

(1) "Nature" here and in chap. 5 is "Heaven-Earth."

CHAPTER 8

The highest goodness resembles water. Water greatly benefits all things, but does not assert itself.

He approximates to the Tao, who abides by that which men despise.

He revolutionizes the place in which he dwells; his depth is immeasurable; he strengthens moral qualities by what he bestows; he augments sincerity by what he says; he evokes peace by his administration; his transactions manifest ability, he is opportune in all his movements.

Forasmuch as he does not assert himself he is free from blame.[1]

Comment

Water adapts itself to every mold and flows into any vessel, making no difference between the clean and the foul, the fine and the coarse. In the words of Ruskin: "Of all inorganic substances, acting in their own proper nature, and without assistance or combination, water is the most wonderful." Hence it is the fittest type of the highest goodness, which by its self-abandon and eagerness to serve, has always been the world's chief puzzle. "Then said I, lo! I am come: in the roll of the Book it is written of Me, I delight to do Thy Will, O my God; yea, Thy law is within my heart." (Ps. xl, 7.) It is the universal solvent of man's ills. "Whosoever drinketh of the water that I shall give him shall never thirst; but the water that I shall give him shall become in him a well of water springing up into eternal life." (John. iv, 14.) The most wretched and the most outcast may here find satisfaction for their needs. "And both the Pharisees and the Scribes murmured, saying, This man receiveth sinners, and eateth with them." (Luke xv, 2.)

Note

(1) There is a correspondence between early Chinese thought and the beginning of Greek philosophy. Thales, born only some thirty odd years before Lao-tzu, and who, like him, was a seeker after wisdom, is said to have "maintained water to be the ground of all things," but while Thales appears to have confined his philosophy to the conclusions that as it is water or moisture which keeps the world alive, so there is in man and in all things a living power which prevents them becoming mere heaps of dead atoms. Lao-tzu goes further and draws from the non-assertion of water the inference that the highest goodness, that which alone can transform the world, must, like water, be born of that power which is the child of purity—the purity of selflessness.

Lao-tzu's teaching is expanded with great force and beauty in a later Taoist treatise *History of the Great Light, Taoist Texts,* by Balfour.

CHAPTER 9

It is better to leave alone, than to grasp at fullness.

Sharpness, which results from filing, cannot be preserved.

None can protect the hall that is filled with gold and jade.

Opulence, honors, pride, necessarily bequeath calamity.

Merit established, a name made, then retirement —this is the way of Heaven.[1]

Comment

"A man is rich in proportion to the number of things he can afford to let alone," says Thoreau.

"In praying, use not vain repetitions as the Gentiles do." "When ye fast, be not as the hypocrites of a sad countenance; for they disfigure their faces, that they may be seen of men to fast." Such "grasping at fulness" had better be left alone.

"Meat will not commend us to God: neither, if we eat not, do we lack." Asceticism which begins and ends on the surface leaves the heart without permanent trace; it is a sharpness which is filed; it leads to self-assertion, to pride and to disputations. "Each one of you saith, I am of Paul; and I of Apollos; and I of Cephas; and I of Christ." Minds full of names and parties are as vulnerable as a "hall filled with gold and jade."

Honors are shadowed by calamities; therefore "I thank God that I baptized none of you. . . . We are fools for Christ's sake. . . . While we look not at the things which are seen, but at the things which are not seen: for the things which are seen are temporal; but the things which are not seen are eternal."

"Merit established, a name made, then retirement—this is the way of heaven."

Note

(1) Literally—"Heaven's Tao."

CHAPTER 10

By steadily disciplining the animal nature, until it becomes one pointed, it is possible to establish the Indivisible.[1]

By undivided attention to the soul, rendering it passive,[2] it is possible to become as an infant child.[3]

By purifying the mind of phantasms,[4] it is possible to become without fault.[5]

By perfecting the people, and pacifying the empire, it is possible to prove non-attachment.[6]

By functioning on the supra-physical planes,[7] it is possible to be independent of the lower mind.[8]

By making intuition omniscient,[9] it is impossible to discard knowledge.[10]

Producing! Nourishing! Developing, without self-consciousness! Acting, without seeking the fruit! Progressing, without thinking of growth! This is the abyss of energy.[11]

Comment

Long and steep is the road man has to travel; great the distance between the animalness of the undeveloped man, knowing no motive but the gratification of desire, and the purity of the saint, whose senses center in the One. Well might Chuang Tzu say, "The whole of life is a round of incessant solicitude, its duties are never finished." Moreover, the arena where effort will be most successful lies in those dim and formless regions of our wondrous selves, where a formative process is ever going on controlling the character of the thoughts we put into words. No language can express it. Lao-tzu has stated the problem as clearly as it can be framed in speech.

If, however, the ascent be difficult, the summit is glorious. In the beginning, a discontented, wayward, wilful child; in the end, a God, performing all duties, yet never leaving the eternal home, where calm peace and joy unspeakable reign evermore. Such the destiny, such the reward of him who fathoms perfection's abyss. "He that overcometh, I will give to him to sit down with me in my throne, as I also overcame, and sat down with my Father in his throne." (Rev. iii, 21.)

Notes

(1) i. e.: The spiritual self, becoming permanently self-conscious on its own plane. Very little is said in the Confucian classics on this line. The Confucian is scarcely conscious of the distinction between soul and body.

(2) The danger is that the separated essence will set up a separated will. Conversely the way to perfection is submission to the simplicity of the eternal purity.

(3) An infant has always been the symbol of the initiate, or one who has been re-born. Compare the conversation of Jesus with Nicodemus. (John iii, 1-5.)

(4) Namely: Living a life of abstract thought; ever regarding the thought as more important than the act, or, as Jacob Böhme would say, "forsaking all to become like All."

(5) "It is necessary in attending to the affairs of life to be very careful of those thoughts which appear insignificant and trifling, lest they find a permanent lodging in the mind. If they are retained in the heart there is a disease in the vitals, which no medicine can cure."—*Kuan Yin Tzu.*

(6) Anyone practicing the yoga of the three first sentences could only accept the office of ruler as a sacrifice to duty, and the acceptance would prove the reality of his non-attachment.

(7) Literally—"opening and shutting heaven's gates." "There not infrequently occur individuals so constituted that the spirit can perceive independently of the corporal organs, or can, perhaps, wholly or partially quit the body for a time and return to it again."—*Alfred Wallace,* F. R. S.

(8) Literally—"The Female Bird." The bird Karshipta, in Hindu mythology, represents the human mind-soul.

(9) Possible only by steady and prolonged concentration on the inner world.

(10) i.e.: Information acquired by the ordinary processes of study and research. The individual being separated from the universal only by differentiation, his limitations grow less in proportion to his approximation to and union with

the divine. The idea is again and again expressed by the old Greek philosophers, the Indian Yogis, Neo-Platonists, as well as by Jacob Böhme and Swedenborg. Su-cheh gives the following illustration: "A mirror reflects whatever fronts it, and does so unconsciously; the beginning of error is the putting of self to the fore."

(11) The three first sentences deal with the purity of the inner; the three next with the purity of the outer, while the seventh describes the purity of the whole—the invisibility or interiorness of godliness.

"If, therefore, thine eye be single, thy whole body shall be full of light."   (Matt. vi, 22.)

CHAPTER 11

Thirty spokes meet in one hub, but the need for the cart existed when as yet it was not. Clay is fashioned into vessels, but the need for the vessel existed when as yet it was not. Doors and windows are cut to make a house, but the need for the house existed when as yet it was not. Hence there is a profitableness in that which is and a need in that which is not.[1]

Comment

The advantage does not lie in the nature of the thing itself, but in that which the user brings to it. A book may prove the salvation of one, the damnation of another. "Cast not your pearls before swine." "Give not that which is holy unto the dogs." "For you therefore which believe is the preciousness: but for such as disbelieve . . . a stone of stumbling and a rock of offense."

Notes

(1) This chapter teaches that the real usefulness of everything lies in the original noumenal conception.

Hsüeh-kün-ts'ai says: "Although substance and the accidental are ever changing places, the intention is to make that which is the visible [accident] express that which is invisible [substance]. Everyone knows the advantage of the visible, but who searches for the usefulness of the invisible, and hence Lao Tzu illustrates the matter as in the text."

Says Tung-tei-ning: "This chapter shows that while substance has form its usefulness lies in its essence; the noumenal and the phenomenal (lit. the empty and the real) continually revolve around each other, but while the latter has the advantage of being existent, its root lies in that which is (apparently) non-existence, and it is that which constitutes its usefulness." Cf. Notes to ch. 1.

Su-cheh has the following: "The ends of matter have been reached when it has been fashioned into form, but the usefulness of the form lies both in the phenomenal and in the noumenal. When it is not on the phenomenal plane it is on the noumenal, and its usefulness lies in its noumenon. When it is not on the noumenal plane it is on the phenomenal, and its profitableness is manifested by phenomena."

This teaching concerning the relations between concealed and revealed nature was also enunciated by Paracelsus; it is elaborated in the Samkhya philosophy of India; and was taught by the Hermetic philosophers of Greece.

Compare also the following explanation by Leibnitz: "The primitive element of every material body being force, which has none of the characteristics of matter—it can be conceived but can never be the object of any imaginative representation."

Vide *The Secret Doctrine,* vol. 1, p. 303; also chap. 49 of the *Tao-teh-king,* where the reality of the phenomenal universe is described as units meeting in unity—immaterial.

CHAPTER 12

The five colors blind men's eyes.[1]
The five tones deafen men's ears.[2]
The five flavors blunt men's appetites.[3]
Galloping and hunting derange men's minds.[4]
Articles which are rare limit the freedom of men's actions.[5]
On this account the holy man regards the stomach and not the eye.[6]
He puts aside the one, that he may take the other in hand.[7]

Comment

What is born of the senses stupefies more than it stimulates. Man realizes himself only as he polarizes his sense organs in the spiritual, even as his spiritual faculties are polarized in the material; in other words, as he overcomes "the terrible spirit of duality within," described in Rom. vii, and prayed against in the invocation, "Lead us not into temptation," for the rainbow hues of earth blind the eyes to the translucent glories of heaven, its harmonies drown heaven's melodies, its viands spoil the taste for the flavor of the "Bread of Life," and hence, the sage, who, in the language of Paul, is "dead unto sin, but alive unto God," turns from the sensuous to the supersensuous, passes from the narrow boundaries of the material to the limitless expanse of the spiritual.

> "Look not thou on beauty's charming,
> Sit thou still when kings are arming,
> Taste not when the wine cup glistens,
> Speak not when the people listens,
> Stop thine ear against the singer,
> From the red gold keep thy finger,
> Vacant heart, and hand, and eye,
> Easy live and quiet die."
> —Walter Scott.

Said Thomas à Kempis in his *The Imitation of Christ:*

"Fly the tumult of the world as much as thou canst, . . . for we are quickly defiled and enthralled by vanity." *The five colors blind men's eyes.*

Notes

(1) Namely: Blue, yellow, white, black, red. *Tung-tei-ning* notes that the more the eyes see the more they desire. Cf. Eccles. i, 8.

(2) "Strauss says that the five sounds in old Chinese were, C, D, E, G, A, and that they were the same with the five notes of old Scotch airs. The notes F and B are avoided."— *China Review*. vol. 13, p. 12.

(3) Namely: Sour, salt, sweet, tart, bitter. Cf. Eccles. vi, 7.

(4) "Desire is limitless and the cause of all trouble," says Tung-tei-ning. (Cf. ch. 64.)

(5) "Because," says Wang-pi, "they lead men away from the straight path into byways full of obstacles."

(6) "The stomach serves, the eye demands service; therefore, the Sage discards the eye." is Wang-pi's explanation.

Wu-ch'eng says that when the spirit becomes dyed with the colors of the physical world, and feels impelled to investigate it, even to its frontiers, it loses its balance. It is because it is the eye that is chiefly the cause of this deflection that the chapter begins and ends with a condemnation of that organ.

Su-cheh aptly remarks that while the eye covets more than it retains, the stomach desires no more than it requires.

(7) Lit.—He withdraws from this and accepts that. Wang-pi sums up the teaching of this sevenfold chapter thus: "When the ears, eyes, mouth and mind are subservient to the soul, all is well; but when it is otherwise, the spontaneity of man's nature is disturbed."

Chuang-tzu says: "A man who plays for counters will play well. If he stake his girdle (in which he keeps his loose cash), he will be nervous; if yellow gold, he will lose his wits. His skill is the same in each case, but he is distracted by the value of his stake. And everyone who attaches importance to the external becomes internally without resource." *Chuang Tzu,* by H. A. Giles.

"The teaching of Lao-tsze comes here, and in the 13th chapter very near to that of Buddha."—J. Edkins, *China Review,* vol. 13, 12.

CHAPTER 13

Equally fear favor and disgrace.

Regard a great calamity as you do your own body.

What is meant by "Equally fear favor and disgrace?" Favor should be disparaged. Gained or lost it arouses apprehension. Hence it is said, "Equally fear favor and disgrace."

What is meant by "Regard a great calamity as you do your own body?" Why have I any sense of misfortune? Because I am conscious of myself. Were I not conscious of my body, what distresses should I have?

Therefore, it is only they who value their persons because of their obligations, who may be entrusted with the empire. It is only they who love themselves on account of their responsibilities, who may be charged with the care of the state.[1]

Comment

"Wherefore if any man is in Christ, he is a new creature; the old things are passed away; behold, they are become new." (II Cor. v, 17) When the consciousness is identified no longer with the self, but with the Christ, the whole world is changed; even the conceptions of fear and favor disappear—these arise with "the conception of the I." When freed by the Truth (John viii, 31, 32) man is no more attached to form, because living in faith, "the faith which is in the Son of God" (Gal. ii, 20), then his untrammeled spirit rises above the illusions of pain, sorrow and disaster. He "lives neither in the present nor the future, but in the eternal." He "recognizes this individuality as not himself, but that thing which he has with pain created for his own use, and by means of which he purposes, as his growth slowly develops his intelligence, to reach to the life beyond individuality."—*Light on the Path.*

Note

(1) Text and comment have evidently become mixed here. Probably the two first sentences alone are Lao-tzu's, and the rest the later addition of a commentator.

CHAPTER 14

Looked for but invisible—it may be named "colorless."[1]

Listened for, but inaudible—it may be named "elusive."[2]

Clutched at but unattainable—it may be named "subtile."[3]

These three cannot be unraveled by questioning, for they blend into one.[4]

Neither brighter above, nor darker below.

Its line, though continuous, is nameless, and in that it reverts to vacuity.

It may be styled "The form of the formless"; "The image of the imageless"; in a word—"The indefinite."[5]

Go in front of it and you will discover no beginning; follow after and you will perceive no ending.[6]

Lay hold of this ancient doctrine; apply it in controlling the things of the present day,[7] you will then understand how from the first it has been the origin of everything.[8]

Here, indeed, is the clue to the Tao.[9]

Comment

Every name of God and each attribute are but shadows of the Reality, limited manifestations of the Limitless, as time is an attribute of Eternity, mind an attribute of Consciousness, flame an attribute of Fire. "Dwelling in light unapproachable" is Paul's description. (I Tim. vi, 16.)

Notes

(1) Because in It all colors are equalized.
(2) Because in It all sounds are harmonized.

(3) Within It is all form, yet It is formless.

(4) Three metaphysical hypostases, but one in essence, the unit of all consciousnesses, personified by the Hindus as Ishvara. The passage bears a close resemblance to Mesopotamian thought. The idea of a trinity in unity is a conception common to all religions, ancient or modern. Without the concrete ideas of substance, life and motion, even an abstract concept of the Divine is impossible.

(5) Cf. the Akhmin Codex, translated in *Fragments of a Faith Forgotten,* by G. R. S. Mead.

(6) Cf. the shloka quoted by Dr. Annie Besant in *Seven Great Religions:*—"When there is no darkness, neither day nor night, neither being nor non-being, there is Shiva alone. He is indestructible. He is to be adored by Savitri, from him alone comes forth the ancient wisdom. Not above, nor below, nor in the midst can he be comprehended, nor is there any similitude for him whose name is infinite glory. Not by the sight is established his form; none beholds him by the eye. Those who know him by the heart and the mind, dwelling in the heart, become immortal."

(7) "Employ the ancient doctrine of non-attachment to action, to govern the present period of continuous action."— *Tung-tei-ning.*

(8) Of the evil as well as of the good. Cf. Isa. xlv, 7. *Amos.* iii, 6.

(9) viz.: Building the invisible into the visible. Said a Christian writer in the Middle Ages "Praying will either make a man leave off sinning, or sinning will make a man leave off praying."

CHAPTER 15

Profound indeed were the most excellent among the ancients, penetrating, fathomless; inasmuch as they were fathomless it becomes necessary to employ far fetched symbols when speaking of them.

Irresolute—as if fording a stream in winter.

Timid—as though fearful of their neighbors.

Grave—as if they were guests.[1]

Elusive—like ice about to melt.

Simple—like raw material.[2]

Expansive—like the space between hills.

Turbid—like muddy water.[3]

Who can still the turbid and make it gradually clear; or quiet the active so that by degrees it shall become productive? Only he who keeps this Tao, without desiring fullness. If one is not full it is possible to be antiquated and not newly fashioned.[4]

Comment

The innerness of no faith can be reached unless there is a profound sympathy with its devotees, the public statements often being but veils, hiding more than they reveal. This was so in Egypt, Greece, Rome, India and Persia; even the Aborigines of Central Australia today have their secret rites and doctrines revealed only to the males of the tribe after passing the manhood tests, and rigidly concealed, not only from the outside world, but from their own women and children. Jesus talked in parables to the crowd, explanations were reserved for his disciples. In the early Christian centuries truths unspoken in the public pulpits were revealed to a *disciplina arcani*. So also Lao-tzu is more impressed with the reticence of the ancients than with their eloquence. Only that self-restrained silence, born of "the peace of God, which passeth all understanding," and which seeks no earthly "fulness," can clear turbidity and make outward activity wholly productive without any destructive element. For such a storm is as a calm, or the echo of distant music.

Notes

(1) Chinese etiquette requires that a guest shall preserve due gravity in the presence of his host, to express his consciousness that he is where he is not himself a master, and must therefore guard himself.

(2) "Simplicity is the highest quality of expression. It is that quality to which art comes in its supreme moments. It marks the final stage of growth. It is the rarest, as it is the most precious, result which men secure in their self-training."

(3) This seven-fold illustration marks a certain progression—1. There is uncertainty of purpose. 2. The naturally resultant timidity of expression. 3. Yet a consciousness of a certain kind of standing. 4. But the position allows of no self assertion. 5. Nevertheless there is an inner center round which the whole man focuses his strength. 6. And from this inner center of self-consciousness there springs an all-embracing comprehensiveness. 7. This comprehensiveness because including All is as No-Thing (*"Turbid—like muddied water."*)

(4) All external conditions alike. Old age as serviceable as youth; youth as fruitful as old age.

CHAPTER 16

Abstraction complete, quiescence maintained unalloyed,[1] the various forms arise with one accord, and I observe that each returns again.[2] All things thrive and increase, then each returns again to the root.[3] This return to the root is called "stillness,"[4] or it may be described as a return to report that they have fulfilled their destiny. This report is called "the unchanging rule."[5]

Knowledge of this unchanging rule is called "illumination." Those who are ignorant of it give way to abandon and to recklessness.

Knowledge of this unchanging rule leads to toleration.

Toleration leads to comprehension.[6]

Comprehension leads to sovereignty.[7]

Sovereignty leads to heaven-likeness.

Heaven-likeness leads to the Tao.

The Tao leads to continuity.

Though the body be no more, there is then no danger.[8]

Comment

Plato says: "When a man is always occupied with the cravings of desire and ambition, and is eagerly striving to satisfy them, all his thoughts must be mortal, and, as far as it is possible altogether to become such, he must be mortal every whit, because he has cherished his mortal part. But he who has been earnest in the love of knowledge and of true wisdom, and has exercised his intellect more than any other part of him, must have thoughts immortal and divine, if he attain truth, and in so far as human nature is capable of sharing in immortality, he must be altogether immortal; and since he is ever cherising the divine power, and has the divinity within him in perfect order, he will be perfectly happy."[9]

"Knowledge of the Unchanging Rule," says Lao-tzu, is the first step, namely, detachment from the external, even as Nature sacrifices its objective existence to retire whence it came and announce the purport of its forthcoming fulfilled. In the language of one of the Upanishads, "When all the bonds of the heart are broken, then the man becomes immortal. *Though the body be no more, there is then no danger.*"

Notes

(1) Su-cheh observes that neither abstraction nor quiescence are complete unless unconscious. So long as they are maintained with effort there can be neither absolute abstraction nor perfect stillness.

(2) "I think that what struck Lao Tzu was the fact that vegetable life seemed to be controlled by the quiet and invisible root: from it everything comes forth as having received a commission: to it there is a return, as if reporting the fulfillment of the commission."—J. P. Maclagan.

(3)   "That each, who seems a separate whole,
        Should move his rounds, and fusing all
        The skirts of self again, should fall
        Remerging in the general soul."   —Tennyson

(4) The word here translated, "stillness," is the same as that rendered "quiescence" in the first sentence, suggesting a similitude between the ideal rest of the soul and the rest or pralaya of the vegetable kingdom.

(5) "As thousands of sparks rise from the fire, and then again merge into the fire; as clouds of dust rise in the air, and then rest again in the dust; as thousands of bubbles rise in the rivers, and melt into water again; in the same way from non-being come forth beings, and merge in Him again."—*Central Hindu College Magazine,* May, 1902.

(6) The submergence of the personal I into the impersonal All.

(7) Complete sway over desire.

(8) Because no longer bound to earth, "which time is wont to prey upon."
See II. Cor. v. 1. Also *The Secret Doctrine* (3d ed.) vol. 3, 454.

(9) *Timaeus.* Jowett's translation, vol. 3, p. 513.

CHAPTER 17

First the supreme. Then a sense of separateness. Next preferences and eulogies. Lastly, fear. Then scorn.[1]

Hence it is plain that lack of sincerity has its origin in superficial faith.

Cautious! They valued their words,[2] accomplished their purposes, settled their affairs, and the people all said: "We are spontaneous."[3]

Comment

In Eden, man at first had no consciousness of himself. He was untempted because without personal desire. It was the contemplation of the fruit as of something which had the power of pleasing, which gave birth to the idea of caring and striving for that phenomenal self whose reflection finds its center in our emotions and judgments. It is the separation of our personalities from our true individuality which arouses within us the sense of conflict. *First the Supreme; then a sense of separateness.* Preferences, eulogies, fear, scorn, are inevitable results. At this stage man loses his power over nature. "Thorn and thistles" grow apace. Duty becomes labor. The curse is pronounced—"In the sweat of thy face shalt thou eat bread."

How shall the *status quo ante* be attained? By retracing the false steps. Contemplation of the true and eternal must revive and nourish the lost faith. The emotions must be brought under control, so that no excess of feeling shall cause the mouth to exaggerate or distort truth. Words must be weighed, so that there shall ever be a proper relation between the spoken speech and the person to whom it is addressed. By sympathetic insight, which looks at everything from the viewpoint of the other, and speaks accordingly, one's purposes will be accomplished, and those affected by us helped and not hindered. Without understanding why, the whole neighborhood will be benefited. *"And the people all said, We are natural."*

"Let every man be swift to hear, slow to speak, slow to wrath. If any man thinketh himself to be religious, while he bridleth not his tongue, but deceiveth his heart, this man's religion is vain. For in many things we all stumble. If any stumble not in word, the same is a perfect man, able to bridle the whole body also." (Ias. I, 19: 26; III, 2)

Notes

(1) The various stages of descent into matter. Students will recall the well-known Gnostic phrase, "the falling down of the Aeons."

(2) "The ancients were slow of speech, lest in their acts they should not come up to what they said. The wise man is slow of utterance, but diligent in action."—Confucius.

(3) Chuang-tzu aptly describes the mass of mankind as babes who receive "the benefits of a mother's care without troubling themselves to think to whom they are indebted for them."

CHAPTER 18

The great Tao faded and there was benevolence and righteousness. Worldly wisdom and shrewdness appeared and there was much dissembling.[1]

The family relationships no longer harmonious, there was filial piety and paternal love.

The state and the clans in anarchy, there was loyalty and faithfulness.[2]

Comment

The so-called monotheistic peoples are as idolatrous as the most polytheistic. The former love their idols, the latter fear them. The graven images of the one often consecrate their sin; the worshiped virtues of the other consolidate their vice. Virtues and duties are separative, subtle forms of self-assertion, something lower than that ideal of ideals which identifies itself with the All, and in the joy of service annihilates self. Benevolence, righteousness, filiality, paternalism, loyalty, devotion, is each in its own way a degenerate, when The Tao, the Great Ideal, The One Life, recedes from view. Woe to that captain who, when navigating his vessel into port, allows the various lights and sounds of the harbor to turn his attention from the flashing signals of the lighthouse. To know true monotheism, meditate on lives such as Buddha and Jesus—from these consciousnesses The Great Tao never faded.

"For the love of Christ constraineth us; because we thus judge, that one died for all, therefore all died; and He died for all, that they which live should no longer live unto themselves, but unto Him who for their sakes died and rose again." (II Cor. v, 14-15.)

Notes

(1) The spiritual intuition of the primitive ages—"the Golden Age" described by Plato in the fourth book of his *Laws*—having vanished, ethical science in which the

phantasms of righteousness, benevolence, etc., loomed large became the vogue. The omnipresent Unity, the great Tao, having disappeared, the veil of Maya showed multiple minor reflections, and these shadows being mistaken for substance the evils mentioned in the text arose, because, to borrow the explanation of the commentator, Kuan-yin-tzu, "Although in themselves true, these moral qualities, when substitutes for the Tao, become false."

(2) Given a normal condition of affairs and obedience and love in the family, loyalty and faithfulness in the State, may be taken for granted, as the ceaseless beating of the heart, or the continual flow of blood through the healthy body. The special mention therefore of loyalty and love indicate disease.

CHAPTER 19

Abandon knowledge, discard wisdom—the people will gain a hundred fold.

Abandon the humanities, discard righteousness—the people will return to filial love.

Abandon cleverness, discard gain—robbers and thieves will be no more.[1]

These three,[2] being considered not sufficiently aesthetic, therefore many other devices[3] were added. Better observe simplicity,[4] encourage primitiveness, lessen the number of private projects, and moderate desire.[5]

Comment

Whether on the physical or spiritual planes, disintegration is essential to progression. However good the ritual, it should be cast aside once the life has outgrown the form. In passing from infancy to old age, mankind proceeds from multiplicity to simplicity, from activity to quiescence, and this natural physical law is also the path for the soul. The desires fade, or are perhaps absorbed, as the orb of truth rises.

"The wisdom of this world is foolishness with God," says Paul.

"Except ye fast to the world, ye shall in no wise find the kingdom of God," is one of the forgotten sayings of the Christ.

Notes

(1) Virtues which are exotics and not habitats are dangerous freaks, diverting the mind from inner realities. The teaching is eloquently set forth by J. B. of *The Christian World*. "What a remove," . . . he writes, "from the thing we call 'cleverness,' the element which made Jesus supreme in the hearts of his followers! Was it by 'cleverness' that, in Ullmann's striking words, 'His mere presence passed a

silent but irresistible sentence upon those by whom he was surrounded?' Was it a mere trick of the intellect that his look could break a strong man's heart? In this highest example we have demonstration of the fact that the crowning endowment of humanity is beyond and behind intellect, using that only as a tool. . . . We are in an age of culture and of general knowledge grinding. More than ever necessary is that for every teacher, but it is only a beginning. Our qualification for any grade of spiritual office is in the incessant cultivation of our central innermost. It is when we find our Higher Self, our greater Ego, the infinite Ground of our being, to be more and more filling us and making our life, that we can speak of progress."

(2) Namely: The three duplicates, knowledge, wisdom; benevolence, righteousness; cleverness, gain. Standing alone they are painted fruits which arouse expectations but fail to satisfy hunger. Cf. Matt. xxi. 17-19.

(3) Once let the outer usurp the inner, and, like uncontrolled competition in business, it will end in bankruptcy.

(4) Tsaio-ju-ho observes that primitive simplicity embraces the very essence of knowledge, wisdom, benevolence and righteousness.

(5) The way of the Christ, as of all great religious leaders, is to discourage monopoly and practice spiritual socialism.

See notes to chap. 38.

CHAPTER 20

Scholarship abandoned, sorrow vanishes.[1]
Yes and yea, are they not almost alike?
Goodness and evil, are they not akin?[2]
Untrammeled and without limits—yet that may not be lightly esteemed which all men reverence.[3]
The multitude are joyful and merry—as though feasting on a day of sacrifice, or ascending a high tower in spring.[4] I alone am anchored without giving any sign[5]—like an infant, undeveloped.
My homeless heart wanders among the things of sense, as if it had nowhere to stay.
The multitude have enough and to spare[6]—I alone am as one who has lost something.
Have I then the mind of a fool? Am I so very confused?
Ordinary men are bright enough. I alone am dull.
Ordinary men are full of excitement. I alone am heavy-hearted.
Boundless as the sea, drifting to and fro, as if without a place to rest.[7]
All men have some purpose. I alone am thick-headed as a boor.[8]
I am alone—differing from others, in that I reverence and seek the Nursing Mother.[9]

Comment

Says the *Theologia Germanica:* "He who is without the sense of sin must be either Christ or the evil spirit." It is questionable, perhaps, if such an affirmation would bear a thorough philosophical sifting, but it is certain that the consciousness of insufficiency and failure is the first step toward the noble and worthy, as distinct from what is simply innocent and pure, and that life is a failure which, drifting with the crowd, knows nothing of aloneness, because it lacks stamina to resist absorption.

Though, therefore, we find Lao-tzu in advance of his fellows, bewailing that he is alone among men, we may be sure that he was not always so, and that if he at the last stood apart from his fellows, it was because he had exhausted the pleasures the world was able to afford. Experience had made him wise, but how had he attained this wisdom? By contemplation of the Tao, which for him took the place of the Christ, who had not then come. He saw the promise, greeted it from afar, and confessed himself a stranger and a pilgrim on the earth. (See Heb. xi, 13.)

Is not the Christ "that side of the nature of God which has expressed itself in creation?" (See Col. i, 16-17.) Even so for Lao-tzu the "Nursing Mother," whom he reverenced, was the Tao manifested, the Eternal revealed in his works. It is the contemplation of this sacred mystery, the cross in the heart of God, that leads penitents to the Father's feet. It was the contemplation of this same mystery, the oneness of the divine with all human joys and sorrows, that condemned Lao-tzu to the noble loneliness of which the present chapter is an echo.

If our reasoning be sound we see how the atonement occupies a natural place in the scheme of things; and that all great souls, of all faiths, have come to God by one road, namely, by perceiving the oneness of God with men in their triumphs and failures. It was this insight into the union of the finite with the infinite that made Lao-tzu alone in his generation: *"I am alone, differing from others, in that I reverence and seek the Nursing Mother."* It was this which enabled him to see below the surface, to discover that in time, in earth, and in self there is neither satisfaction, joy nor peace. And like all who have traveled this road he paid the penalty of aloneness, lived on high planes of thought, unexplored by his less advanced contemporaries. Such loneliness is, however, its own reward. The electric wire derives its usefulness from its insulation. An adulterated message would result from too close a fellowship with men.

Notes

(1) Was not "the desire to know" the very beginning of tears?

59

"A humble knowledge of thyself is a surer way to God than a deep search after learning."—*Imitation of Christ,* bk. i. ch. 3.

(2) What use is there in further talk of my way and your way, of this view and that? The right and the wrong way are things which concern the minds only of those who are groping in the dark. To the Sage sitting in the full light of heaven, the difference between No and Yes is not much after all. These are distinctions and things of prejudice, and he is not concerned with them."—W. R. Old in *The Theosophical Review,* vol. 31, p. 68.

"Demon est Deus inversus." See *The Secret Doctrine,* vol. 1, section xi. (All references are to the 3 vol. ed., 1893.)

(3) Su-cheh explains this passage to mean that though the Sage (Holy Man) has escaped from Maya, or the illusion of egoism, he does not on that account overlook the distinctions of society, but gives honor to whom honor is due, acknowledges authority, yet comes under the power of none. (Comp. John viii, 37.)

(4) "Spring is the time of the union of the male and female principles; all things are thus moved. He who ascends a tower to gaze has his will as it were depraved."—P. J. Macglagan.

(5) Literally "without omens" i.e., without indications from the sensuous world.

(6) "Superabundance, i.e., as if they had ability and wisdom more than enough for themselves, on the strength of which they there rush out in various lines of activity."—P. J. Macglagan.

(7) Contrasting himself with the recluses of his day Confucius said: "I am different from these. I have no course for which I am predetermined and no course against which I am predetermined." (*Analects,* xviii. ch. 8:5)

(8) See I. Cor. iv, 9-13.

(9) "I have not so far left the coasts of life
To travel inland, that I cannot hear
That murmur of the outer Infinite
Which unweaned babies smile at in their sleep
When wondered at for smiling."

E. B. Browning in *Aurora Leigh.*

The saddened tone of this chapter, so different from the general character of the work, recalls one of the *Logia* discovered in Egypt by Grenfell and Hunt in 1896: "Jesus saith, I stood in the midst of the world, and in the flesh was I seen of them, and I found all men drunken and none found I athirst among them, and my soul grieveth over the sons of men, because they are blind in their heart."— *Sayings of our Lord.*

CHAPTER 21

The comprehensiveness of supreme energy is its conformity to the Tao.[1]

The Tao considered as an entity is impalpable, indefinite. Indefinite, impalpable, within are conceptions. Impalpable, indefinite, within are shapes.[2] Profound, obscure, within is the essence. This essence being supremely real, within is sincerity.

From the beginning until now it has not changed,[3] and thus it has watched all the essentials. How do I know it has been thus with all principles? By what has just been said.

Comment

As the gospels, filled with the presence of the Master, preserve no notes of the disciples' sermons, so the true mystic sees God alone in the universe. Is not the spiritual the home of the physical? Is not conformity to the Tao the comprehensiveness of the Energy which is supreme? "In Him we live and move and have our being." "It is His fullness that filleth all in all." "And by Him all things consist." "But the Lord is in his holy temple: be silent before him all the earth."

Notes

(1) See ch. 38.
(2) "The cosmos is all-formed—not having forms external to itself, but changing them itself within itself. Since, then, cosmos is made to be all-formed, what may its maker be? For that, on the one hand, He should not be void of all form; and, on the other hand, if He's all-formed, He will be like the cosmos. Whereas, again, has He a single form, He will thereby be less than cosmos. What, then, say we He is?—that we may not bring our sermon into doubt; for naught that mind conceives of God is doubtful. He,

then, hath one *idea,* which is His own alone, which doth not fall beneath the sight, being bodiless, and (yet) by means of bodies manifesteth all (ideas). And marvel not that there's a bodiless idea." *The Mind to Hermes,* by G. R. S. Mead, in *The Theosophical Review,* vol. 33, p. 52.

(3) Lit.—"Its Name has not departed." Noumenally the Tao is eternal and unchanging; phenomenally It has a beginning and consequently an end.

CHAPTER 22

To be crooked is to be perfected; to be bent is to be straightened; to be lowly[1] is to be filled; to be senile is to be renewed; to be diminished is to be able to receive; to be increased is to be deluded.[2]

Therefore the Holy Man embraces unity,[3] and becomes the world's model.[4]

He is not self-regarding, therefore he is cognizant.[5]

He is not egotistic, therefore he is distinguished.

He is not boastful, therefore he has merit.

He is not conceited, therefore he is superior.

Inasmuch as he strives with none, there are none in the world able to strive with him.[6]

That ancient maxim—'To be crooked is to become perfected'—was it an idle word? Verily, it includes the whole.[7]

Comment

"Every valley shall be exalted, and every mountain shall be made low; and the crooked shall be made a straight place, and the rough places plain." "Everyone that exalteth himself shall be humbled; and he that humbleth himself shall be exalted." These familair Bible texts voice the teaching of religion in all ages, whether it appear in the garb of the Hindu, the Buddhist, the Jew, or the Christian.

Those who have done most for their fellows have been those who have walked most humbly before their Maker. Selflessness has been their chief characteristic. A child is egotistic. A man is unconscious. Abraham, regarded by the Jew, the Muslim and the Christian, as a saint, bowed in continual humility before Jehovah, ordering his life according to the directions of the Invisible. Sakyamuni left a palace to wear the beggar's robe. Socrates followed the guidance of his daemon. It is to the humility of Confucius that the Chinese point with the most satisfaction. Jesus came not to be ministered unto but to minister, according to his own saying, "Whether is greater, he that sitteth at

meat, or he that serveth? Is not he that sitteth at meat?
I am in the midst of you as he that serveth." *To be lowly
is to be filled.*

Notes

(1) The word rendered here "lowly" means the footsteps
of an ox in which water collects; a hollow; a puddle; a
swamp.

(2) "Self-sufficiency invites damage; humility receives
benefits.'—*Shu-king.*

(3) Lit.—"The One," which Wang-pi explains as "diminished to the uttermost." In *Esoteric Buddhism* we read that
the "supreme controlling cause" "is the same for one man
as for every man, the same for humanity as for the animal
kingdom, the same for the physical as for the astral or deva-
chanic planes of existence."—8th ed. Amer., p. 307.

"The more a man is one within himself and becometh
of single heart, so much the more and higher things doth he
understand without labor; for that he receiveth the light
of wisdom from above"—*On the Imitation of Christ.*

(4) Having yielded himself to the Tao, as Paul to the
cross, "the law in his members." (Rom. vii. 23), or the
passion elements of his nature, obey the "law in his mind";
hence he is the *"world's model."*

(5) "The eye does not look at itself, therefore it sees everything; the mirror never reflects itself, thus it is able to re-
flect images. What time has any who is ever attending
to himself to give to anything else?"—*Su-cheh.*

(6) See ch. 66.

"The unassuming are honorable and illustrious; the humble cannot be surpassed."—*Yi-king.* (The Book of Changes.)

(7) Perfection is impossible without a recognition of the
law that every cause produces its own effects, and that no
effects occur without adequate cause. To this majestic and
immutable law Nature offers unceasing sacrifice. It is Nature's implicit submission to a Will higher than herself
that secures the accuracy of scientific investigation. In like
manner individual perfection is attainable only as there
is absolute obedience to Nature's instructions on all planes.
Hence the assertion of the text that *to be crooked,* or to be
willing to bow the neck to the yoke imposed by the might
of superior Wisdom, *includes the whole.* Cf. Isa. i, 16-20.

CHAPTER 23

Few words are natural.

A whirlwind does not outlast the morning; a deluge does not outlast the day. Who produces these? The Heaven-Earth. If the Heaven-Earth cannot produce lasting phenomena, how much less can man?

Wherefore settling everything in accordance with the Tao, embodying the Tao they become identified with the Tao. Embodying its virtue, they become identified with virtue. Embodying loss, they become identified with loss.

Identified with the Tao, they joyfully accept the Tao; identified with virtue, they joyfully accept virtue; identified with loss, they joyfully accept loss.

If sincerity is lacking it is because of superficial faith.

Comment

Nothing reveals man's slight hold on himself like his unending torrential flow of speech. According to the Apostle James unbridled tongues are signs of irreligious hearts (i. 26). An orderly, calm progression—not sudden spurts of spasmodic eloquence—is the example set by Nature for man's imitation. The whirlwind and the deluge do not last. Man's noisy insincerity is the result of his superficiality. This leads him to often content himself with less than the best, to identify himself with what is positive loss, or with what is a mere reflection of the real. God only speaks in the heart of him who, independent of outward circumstance, dwells "in the secret place of the Most High," "under the shadow of the Almighty." (Psalms xci. 1.) "For thus saith the high and lofty One that inhabiteth eternity, whose name is Holy: I dwell in the high and holy place with him also that is of a contrite and humble spirit, to revive the spirit of the humble, and to revive the heart of the contrite." (Isa. lvii, 15.)

CHAPTER 24

Who tiptoes, totters.[1] Who straddles, stumbles.[2]
The self-regarding cannot cognize; the egotistic are
not distinguished; the boastful are not meritorious;
the self-conceited cannot excel. Such from the standpoint of the Tao are like remnants of food, or para-
sites,[3] which all things probably detest. Hence,
those who possess the Tao are not so.[4]

Comment

In a universe where self-sacrifice is the master law of
life the self-seeker is a blot on the sun, a fog obscuring the
landscape, a cog slowing the wheel of evolution. Yet so
infinite is the divine patience at the heart of things, that,
"from the standpoint of the Tao," parasitical though he be,
the self-seeker is permitted to remain, notwithstanding his
inharmony with the scheme of the world. "The Lord is
not slack concerning his promise, as some count slackness;
but is long suffering to you-ward, not wishing that any
should perish, but that all should come to repentance."
(II Pet. iii, 9.)

Notes

(1) "Besser nicht anfangen, Denn erliegen,"—German
Proverb.

(2) "He who stretches his legs does not walk (easily)."—
James Legge.

(3) Cf. Marcus Aurelius' simile of the man who separates
himself from nature. "He is an abscess on the universe."
Bk. v. ch. ix.

(4) The teaching of the chapter is illustrated by a quotation in the *Doctrine of the Mean*. "It is said in the Book
of Poetry, 'Over her embroidered robe she puts a plain
garment,' intimating a dislike to the display of the ele-
gance of the former. Just so it is the way of the Lordly
Man to prefer concealment, while he every day becomes

more illustrious, and it is the way of the small-minded man to seek notoriety, while he daily goes more and more to ruin."

"A wise man never competes under any circumstances."— Confucius.

CHAPTER 25

There was a completed, amorphous something before the Heaven-Earth was born.[1] Tranquil! Boundless! Abiding alone and changing not! Extending everywhere without risk. It may be styled "the world-mother."[2]

I do not know its name, but characterize it—the Tao. Arbitrarily forcing a name upon it I call it the Great. Great, it may be said to be transitory. Transitory, it becomes remote. Remote, it returns.[3]

The Tao, then, is great; Heaven is great; Earth is great; a king is also great.[4] In space there are four that are great, and the king dwells there as one of them.[5]

Man's standard is the earth. Earth's standard is the Heaven. Heaven's standard is the Tao. The Tao's standard is spontaneity.[6]

Comment

Spontaneity, or action which is natural, and effortless, Lao-tzu's symbol for perfection, has a modern apostle in that master of art critics, John Ruskin. This is what he writes in *Sesame and Lilies:* "All good work is essentially done that way—without hesitation, without difficulty, without boasting; and in the doers of the best there is an inner and involuntary power which approximates literally to the instinct of an animal. Nay, I am certain that in the most perfect human artists reason does *not* supersede instinct, but is added to an instinct as much more divine than that of the lower animals as the human body is more beautiful than theirs." (3rd ed. p. 149.)

Notes

(1) The Tao is neither clear nor misty, high nor low; neither here nor there, good nor evil; as without shape, yet

as having shape, and none know whence It came. Yet It has always existed, and the Heaven-Earth sprang from it.— *Su-cheh*.

(2) Lit. "The Mother-of-all-under-heaven."—*Kundalini*.

(3) From Non-existence the Tao comes into Existence, and returns whence It appeared. In other words Manvantara succeeds Pralaya, and Pralaya follows Manvantara throughout Eternity.

(4) I. Esdras iv, 1-12.

(5) The monarch is only great as he is worthy of being the visible representative of the Invisible Powers, The Four Great Ones (the Lords of Karma). This courtly phraseology conveys a veiled warning to the reigning sovereign that there were those higher than he. The warning is repeated and emphasized in less disguised language in the succeeding chapter.

(6) "If man conform to the (requirements of) the earth he obtains all that he needs; if the earth conform to (the laws of) heaven it becomes fertile; if heaven conform to the Tao it becomes able to fulfill Its functions; if the Tao conform to Spontaneity It realizes Itself. Then that which should be square becomes square, and that which should be round becomes round."—*Wang-pi*.

CHAPTER 26

Lightness has its roots in heaviness. Restlessness has a master in stillness. Therefore, the Holy Man travels all day without leaving the baggage wagon.[1] Surrounded by sensuous enjoyments he remains peaceful and free.

How, then, can the Lord of ten thousand chariots[2] regard his personality as of less importance than his royal trust? By levity he will lose his ministers; by restlessness he will lose his throne.

Comment

The frail leaves of the woods owe their stability to the mountains in which the trees are rooted. It is the mighty flood which is the origin of the fleecy, fleeting clouds in the summer sky. The very conception of "heaviness" would be impossible without the idea of "lightness." Woe to that man whose passing moods have no foundation in a weighty soul. He will be swept as driftwood hither and thither, and never reach port.

All movement starts from rest, and is controlled by the still. It is the quiet river bed which directs the course of the impetuous torrent. The restless wind is scattered by the passive block of masonry. It is the man whose heart is still who comes to the front as one of the world's rulers. Restlessness in the citadel of the soul will overthrow the loftiest prince. Even the Lord Jesus would have become tainted when he ate with publicans and sinners had he possessed no unchanging point of rest within.[3]

> "See, O see, the flashing gold
>   From a thousand suns outglancing,
> See the starry Heavens unrolled,
>   And the skies around me dancing:
> Yet I feel *a softer splendor*,
>   Flowing o'er my heart, like *balm*,
> O how thrilling, and how tender!
>   It is Christ!—Creation's Calm."

Notes

(1) i.e. He never throws aside his gravity.

In the eighth chapter of the first book of the *Analects* we read, "Confucius remarked, If the Wise Man is not serious he will not inspire respect, nor will his learning be solid."

(2) The reigning Sovereign.

(3) I am indebted for these thoughts to Victor von Straus. (See his *Lao-Tsĕ's Tao Te King, loc cit.*)

CHAPTER 27

Good doers leave no tracks.[1] True words have no defects. Skillful plans require no calculations. Able closers need no locks and bars, yet none can open what they shut.[2] Real strength wants no cords, yet none can loose it.[3]

It follows that the Holy Man when helping others, works in accordance with the unchanging goodness. Hence, he rejects none. He does the same when helping nature to develop. Therefore, he rejects nothing. This may be called "obscured perception."[4]

Thus the Good Man is the bad man's instructor; the bad man the Good Man's material. Yet he does not esteem himself a teacher,[5] nor does he love his material.[6]

Although one may be wise, here he is deceived.[7] This is "The Cardinal Mystery."[8]

Comment

The Christ declared that his disciples were the salt of the earth, the light of the world; but salt and light act toward all things with equal impartiality; moreover, the salt, because one with the whole, is unnoticed when the flavors are praised; light is indistinguishable from the landscape which it reveals. "Good doers leave no tracks." It is this universalizing of his heart which gives the Sage his power. One with God he is one with all. The fuel dies that the flame may soar. What would become of man if the atmospheric oxygen insisted on remaining itself? The mother travails in pain that the child may be born. The cross is the center of all—"the symbol, not of separatism, but of universality."

Notes

(1) Matt. vi. 3.
(2) i.e. They are independent of externals.

(3) The paragraph teaches that the most forceful energies operate on the spiritual planes. Prayers are more valuable than gold.

(4) In his dealings with humanity the Sage never departs from the eternal law of the Divine Wisdom, that every cause produces its own effect, and that no effect occurs without an adequate cause. The idea may be illustrated by a verse in section 99 of the Koran: "Whosoever hath wrought an ant's weight of good shall behold it, And whosoever hath wrought an ant's weight of evil shall behold it." (Stanley Poole's translation.)

The "perception" of the Sage is said to be obscured because it regards the hidden law, rather than the immediate gain or immediate loss of the individual. The miracles of the Christ were the phenomena of his ministry of which he thought least.

(5) Says *Su-cheh:* "Though himself unable to forget the world, the Sage is able to let the world forget him."

(6) He radiates power as the sun heat. The Lord Jesus was more concerned to witness for the truth than to save individuals.

(7) Cf. chaps. 20, 58, 73.

(8) Huai-nan-tza illustrates the general teaching of the chapter by two illustrations from Chinese history. The Builder of the Great Wall could not retain the succession to the throne in his family; whereas the descendants of the virtuous Wu Wang swayed the scepter for thirty-four generations.

"Mystery" here reminds us of the Abyss of chap. 1.

CHAPTER 28

One conscious of virility, maintaining muliebrity,[1] is a world-channel. From a world-channel the unchanging energy never departs. This is to revert to the state of infancy.

One conscious of brightness, placid in shade, is a world-model. In a world-model the unchanging energy remains undiminished. This is to revert to the unlimited.

One conscious of merit, content in disgrace, is a world-valley. In a world-valley the unchanging energy is sufficient. This is to revert to simplicity.

Simplicity scattered becomes capacity, and in the hands of the Holy Man, administrators.

Thus the Supreme Mandate may not be sundered.

Comment

True power is the power to be without power. The highest perfection is "infancy," "simplicity"—the surrender of the individual to the universal. Man is greatest when he stoops. The simplicity of the divine is more potent than the multiplied devices of human effort. Do we not read of Wisdom that "being but one she can do all things" (Wisdom of Solomon vii, 27); and did not the Christ choose "little children" as types of His kingdom? That man who is wise enough to emulate the simplicity of the child will, by the purity of his life and the strength of his thought, be an administrator and distributor of spiritual treasure, a great principle and mighty power which no evil force can divide.

In a word, the Kingdom of God will be established when the strong are willing to be weak; when the radiant are satisfied though clouded; when the meritorious though unknown are contented.

"When will Christ's kingdom be realized?" is one of the

questions found in an uncanonical gospel. The answer is "When ye shall trample on the garment of shame, when the two shall be one and the male as the female, neither male nor female." In the end all consciousness of separation will be superseded, a state our author well calls—*the unchanging energy.*

Note

(1) Containing also the feminine qualities.

CHAPTER 29

I perceive that no desire can succeed which has as its objective the moulding of the state. The state possesses a divine capacity, which cannot be moulded.

To make is to mar; to grasp is to lose.

Thus in nature some things lead, others follow; some inspire, others expire; some are strong, some are weak; some survive, others succumb; hence, the Holy Man renounces excess, extravagance, exaltation.[1]

Comment

All power exercised over those who are weaker, whether it is secular or spiritual, is an evil when it subverts natural growth. We can only influence and work no mischief, when we recognize the mysterious subtlety which lies at the root of things, and which cannot be moulded. *Who makes mars; who grasps, loses.*

Notes

(1) The Sage leaves everything to work out its own destiny "Even should a Master—a Jivanmukta, one who has attained union, while still in the body, with that Higher Self—cast the mantle of his power round the disciple, should he wrap him in his aura, even then, it would be of no profit, if the disciple is not ready to burst the veils of his soul with *self-effort*.

"If the nature of the disciple does not respond of its own will, and grow of its own energy, the artificial exaltation would be not only unprofitable but even injurious. For the instant the protecting wall were removed, the reaction would sweep the unprepared neophyte off his feet. . . . And that is why it is so difficult for a Master to interfere with the natural growth of the disciple. . . . Nature must work on in her own way, and growth must proceed from *within without* and never from *without within.*"—*The World-Mystery*, by G.R.S. Mead.

CHAPTER 30

When one uses the Tao in assisting his sovereign, he will not employ arms to coerce the state. Such methods easily react.[1]

Where military camps are established, briers and thorns flourish. When great armies have moved through the land calamities are sure to follow.[2]

The capable are determined, but no more. They will not venture to compel; determined, but not conceited; determined, but not boastful; determined, but not arrogant; determined because it cannot be helped; determined, but not forceful.

When things reach their prime, they begin to age. This cannot be said to be the Tao. What is NOT the Tao soon ends.[3]

Comment

War is crude, unrefined cruelty; a creator of divisions, and an opponent of the unity underlying creation; brute force and strategy are its weapons, each a contradiction of the simplicity and purity of God; its effects extend beyond the physical, and to those who have open ears there come from the Unseen, echoes similar to the lament of the Great Spirit in Hiawatha:

"O my children! my poor children!
Listen to the words of wisdom,
From the lips of the Great Spirit,
From the Master of Life, who made you!"

"I am weary of your quarrels,
Weary of your wars and bloodshed.
Weary of your prayers for vengeance,
Of your wranglings and divisions;
All your strength is in your union,
All your danger is in discord;
Therefore be at peace henceforward,
And as brothers live together,"

Notes

(1) "With what measure ye mete it shall be measured to you again."—Luke vi, 38.

(2) Although the *Tao-Teh-King* is now little read, so manifest is the Law of Retribution that this sentence has become one of the commonest proverbs in the Chinese colloquial.

(3) See chap. 55.

CHAPTER 31

The magnificence of the army cannot make it an auspicious weapon. It is possible that even inanimate Nature detests it. Hence, one who possesses Tao has nothing to do with it.

The Master Thinker (the Sage) when at home honors the left. When leading troops he honors the right. Soldiers are instruments of ill omen. They are not agents for a Master Thinker. Only when it is inevitable will he employ them. What he most prizes is quiet and peace. He will not praise a victory. To do so would show delight in the slaughter of men. As for those who delight in the slaughter of men, the world is too small for the gratification of their desires.

When affairs are felicitous the left is honored, but when they are inauspicious the right is honored. The Second Officer is placed on the left, but the Commander-in-Chief is placed on the right. That is to say, his position is as if he were attending a funeral. The slayer of multitudes should bitterly weep and lament. Having fought and won it is as if he were presiding at a funeral.

Comment

This chapter was doubtless originally a commentary on the preceding section, but subsequently incorporated in the text through the carelessness of a copyist. The language is unlike Lao-tzu's style, and contains one or more anachronisms.

The references to the right and the left will be understood when it is remembered that in China the left is the seat of honor, the right the lower and inferior seat.

Legge remarks that "the concluding sentence will suggest to some readers the words of the Duke of Wellington after Waterloo that to gain a battle was the saddest thing next to losing it."

CHAPTER 32

Tao—the Eternally Nameless.

Though primordial simplicity is infinitesimal, none dare make it a public servant.

Were princes and monarchs able to maintain it, all creation would spontaneously submit.

Heaven and earth harmonized, there would be an abundance of nourishing agencies; the people unbidden, would cooperate of their own accord.

Names arose when differentiation commenced; once there were names it became important to know where to stop. This being known, danger ceased.

The Tao spread throughout the world, may be compared to mountain rivulets and streams flowing toward the sea.

Comment

One Life pervades all, the names by which men identify the phenomenal aspects of The One being but attributes of That. Infinitesimal! It defies analysis but is nevertheless The Force above all forces and in all forces. Were the rulers of earth able to emulate It and so cease to arouse opposition; were they able to maintain this Primordial Simplicity, which being impersonal, generates no force with self-gratification as its objective, everything would be harmonized, for there would be no loss of effort, as there must inevitably be where the full force of action is broken by the personal side wishes of its generator. Then the intellectual and the emotional, the ratiocinative and the spiritual, the aesthetic and the scientific, the strength of the man and the tenderness of the woman, the experience of the adult and the innocence of the child would be diffused into one grand, homogeneous, all-comprehensive consciousness—the whole man, memory, imagination, reason, coordinated and united in the worship of the Unseen. The Tao into whom, in the words of the *Bhagavad Gita,* "all desires flow as rivulets flow into the ocean, which is filled with water, but remaineth unmoved, would be spread throughout the world."

Yet the differences in creation, which have given rise to names, have their uses—danger arises only when man stops at the name, instead of passing on to the Nameless. "And He gave some to be apostles; and some prophets; and some evangelists; and some pastors and teachers; for the perfecting of the saints . . . till we all attain to the unity of the faith . . . unto a full grown man, unto the measure of the stature of the fullness of Christ." (Eph. iv, 11, 13.)

CHAPTER 33

Who knows men has discernment; who knows himself has illumination.[1]

Who overcomes men has strength; who overcomes himself has determination. Who knows contentment has wealth.[2]

Who acts vigorously has will.[3]

Who never departs from his base, endures long; he dies, but does not perish; he lives eternally.[4]

Comment

Immortality is a state to be realized through illumination. "These are they which come out of the great tribulation, and they washed their robes, and made them white in the blood of the Lamb." (Rev. vii, 14.) They ate the flesh and drank the blood of the Son of Man (John vi, 54); and then in turn poured out their own blood for the thirsty and gave their own flesh to the hungry, thus filling up on their part "that which is lacking of the afflictions of Christ." (Col. i, 24.) There is no alkali but this spiritual self-surrender, which finds its meat and its drink in doing the will of the Father (John, iv, 34), which can wash our robes free of the stains of mortality, and make them pure with an incorruptible whiteness. To attain to this not only is it necessary to know men but to know one's Self; not only is contentment required, but a vigorous will, and "He that overcometh shall not be hurt of the second death." (Rev. ii, 11.) E coelo descendit—"From heaven descends (the precept) 'know thyself.' " (Juvenal ii, 27.)

Notes

(1) The discernment which gives knowledge of men by providing points for comparison produces the illumination which leads to self-knowledge. Su-cheh says that one can never know himself until he puts all distinctions on one side; a statement supported by Porphyry, who in his treatise

on sensation says that the mind only sees itself when it regards objects, as "the mind embraces everything, and all that exists is nothing but the mind, which contains bodies of all kinds." See *Encyc. Britt.,* 9th edit., vol. 1., p. 461. Compare also the teachings of Plotinus.

"I, the imperfect, adore my own perfect."—Emerson in his essay *The Oversoul.*

(2) "The Princely Man is contented even in poverty."—*Chinese proverb.* See Phil. iv. 11.

(3) "When I seek nothing from without, but vigorously attend to myself there is nothing which can interfere with my will."—*Su-cheh.*

(4)   "So death, so called, can but the form deface,
     The immortal soul flies out in empty space,
     To seek her fortune in another place."

CHAPTER 34

Supreme is the Tao! All pervasive; it can be on the left hand and on the right.

All things depend on it for life, and it denies none.

Its purposes accomplished, it claims no credit.

It clothes and fosters[1] all things, but claims no lordship.

Ever desireless, it may be named "The Indivisible."

All things revert to it, but it claims no lordship. It may be named "The Supreme."

Because to the end it does not seek supremacy; it is able to accomplish great things.[2]

Comment

Says an unknown pagan quoted by Philoponus—"All things are full of God: on all sides hath He ears, ears that hear, can hear through rocks, and compass earth, and pierce through man himself to hear the smallest thought he hides within his breast."

And says a modern theologian, R. J. Campbell: "The Universe is God living his life, and living it by limitation. But beyond and behind are the infinite resources of his being."

Notes

(1) There is an alternative reading, "lovingly nourishes."

(2) In many editions this sentence refers to the Sage, and not to the Tao. Commenting on the conclusion of the chapter *Su-cheh* says, "Who makes himself great is small." See Matt. xx. 26, 28.

"Whither shall I go from Thy spirit?,
Or whither shall I flee from Thy presence?
If I ascend into heaven, thou art there:

If I make my bed in Sheol, behold, thou art there.
If I take the wings of the morning,
And dwell in the uttermost parts of the sea;
Even there shall Thy hand lead me,
And thy right hand shall hold me."

(Psa. cxxxix. 7-10.)

CHAPTER 35

Apprehend the inimitable conception, you attract the world; coming it receives no harm, but is tranquil, peaceful, satisfied.[1]

Like transient guests, music and dainties pass away.

The Tao entering the mouth is insipid and without flavor; when looked at it evades sight; when listened for it escapes the ear—(yet) its operations are interminable.

Comment

Peace, prosperity, permanence of Empire, are according to the 72nd Psalm (attributed by tradition to Solomon), dependent on the righteousness of the King's rule—who apprehends the Inimitable, The Supreme. "The Hidden Wisdom" (I Cor. ii, 6-30) is omnipotent, "the Alpha and the Omega," the Ruler who directs the destinies of all. YET THIS WHICH IS ALL IS NO-THING.

(Cf. *The Classic of Purity.*)

Note

(1) The text may be read in two ways and it is impossible to say which is correct. It may be rendered as in the translation, or it may be understood thus—"Apprehend the Inimitable Conception. Go throughout the world; go, without harm, you will remain tranquil, peaceful, satisfied." The Chinese may be read either way, and from the viewpoint of the Wisdom both interpretations are equally true.

CHAPTER 36

When about to inhale it is certainly necessary to open the mouth; when about to weaken it is certainly necessary to strengthen; when about to discard it is certainly necessary to promote; when about to take away it is certainly necessary to impart—this is atomic perception.

The weak overcome the strong.

Fish cannot leave the deeps.

The innerness of the government cannot be shown to the people.

Comment

"Though He was a Son, yet (He) learned obedience by the things which He suffered; and having been made perfect, He became unto all them that obey Him the author of eternal salvation." Before the Christ could weaken the pride of the sinner and humble man's false exaltation He had to strengthen and uplift the sinner with the knowledge that He had Himself become for his sake "of no reputation." The intellect may fail to grasp the full meaning of this sacrifice but the spirit knows that its safety lies in surrendering before the surrender of God on its behalf, even as the security of the fish lies in the yielding water.

CHAPTER 37

The Tao—eternally actionless and the cause of all action!

Were princes and monarchs able to acquiesce the myriad existences would by degrees spontaneously transform. Transforming and wishing to function I would immediately guide by the simplicity of the nameless.

The simplicity of the nameless is akin to desirableness.

Desireless and at rest the world would naturally become peaceful.[1]

Comment

The charm of Calvary is the non-attachment and abstention from assertive action of its Central Figure. Free from care for the body or the things of the body, "desireless and at rest," the Lord Jesus became the grain of wheat (Cf. John xii, 24).

Note

(1) Cf. chap. 32.

CHAPTER 38

Superior energy is non-action, hence it is energy.[1]
Inferior energy will not resign action; hence, it is not energy.[2]
Superior energy is actionless because motiveless.
Inferior energy acts from motive.
Superior magnanimity is active but motiveless.[3]
Superior equity is active from motive.
Superior propriety[4] is active;[5] it bares its arm and asserts itself when it meets with no response.[6]
Thus as the Tao recedes there are energies; as the energies recede there is magnanimity; as magnanimity recedes there is equity; as equity recedes there is propriety.[7]
Inasmuch as propriety is the attenuation of conscientiousness it is the origin of disorder.
The beginnings of consciousness are flowers of the Tao, but the commencement of delusion.
Therefore the men who are great[8] live with that which is substantial, they do not stay with that which is superficial; they abide with realities, they do not remain with what is showy. The one they discard, the other they hold.

Comment

The highest energy appears as inaction. To pray the Father in secret is more effective than shouting to the unresponsive crowd. A realization of the "mystery" of the Kingdom, and an understanding of the "riches of the glory" of Christ in the heart is a higher experience than conscious effort to "do all in the name of the Lord Jesus," or even than earnest strife to produce "the fruit of the Spirit." These are excellencies which are indispensable, but they are lights which cast shadows; that which is highest—superior energy—is shadowless. The higher will always result in the lower, but all attempts to build up the lower without the spiritual backing of the higher works as much evil as good. Rudyard Kipling somewhere says, "Good work has nothing to do with, doesn't belong to, the person who does it. It is put into him or her from the outside." Jesus said the same when He declared the kingdom of God to be composed of those who are unconscious of self: "Suffer the little children . . . such' is the kingdom of heaven." "Many will say to me in that day, Lord, Lord, did we not prophesy by thy name, and by thy name cast out demons, and by thy name do mighty works? And then will I profess unto them, I never knew you; depart from Me, ye that work iniquity." (Matt. vii, 22.)

Notes

(1) In this chapter, as elsewhere, though Lao-tzu employs conventional terms, he suggests rather than expresses. "Unto them that are without all things are done in parables." (Mark iv. 11.)

(2) It is the shadow of the infinite in the finite. Superior energy is a ray from the *Name which cannot be named;* inferior energy a ray from the *Tao which can be expressed.* (Cf. ch. 1.) vid. *Chinese Buddhism,* by Joseph Edkins, pp. 371-379.

(3) The old Roman ideal—*"honestas."*

(4) Magnanimity represents energy in manifestation. Elsewhere the character here translated "magnanimity" has been rendered "benevolence."
"Equity" stands for the first differentiation of manifested energy.
"Propriety" represents a still further differentiation, e.g. when the processes of evolution have separated the bird from the fish.

(5) Nothing is said about the inferior qualities because the magnanimity, equity and propriety mentioned in the text, being themselves but reflections, anything inferior would be shadows of shadows.

(6) *Facilis descensus Avernus.*

(7) Observe the difference between Lao-tzu the mystic, and Confucius the moralist. Confucius taught that magna-

nimity and equity were the essentials. Confucius made much of propriety. Men, he said, would attain perfection by pursuing these. Lao-tzu taught that these are but subtle forms of selfishness, and therefore productive of evil, useless shells when the life which they preserved has departed.

The whole chapter, says Paul Carus, "undoubtedly criticizes the Confucian method of preaching ethical culture without taking into consideration the religious emotions." —Lao-tsze's *Tao-teh-king*, p. 306.

(8) "To dwell in the wide house of the world, to stand in the correct seat of the world, and to walk in the great path of the world; when he obtains his desire for office, to practice his principles for the good of the people; and when that desire is disappointed, to practice them alone; to be above the power of riches and honors to make dissipated, of poverty and mean condition to make swerve from principle, and of power and force to make bend—these characteristics constitute the great man."—*Mencius*. (Legge's translation.)

CHAPTER 39

The things which from of old harmonized with the One are: The heavens, which through the One are clear; the earth, which through the One is reposeful; the gods, which through the One are spiritual; space, which through the One is full; whatever has form, which through the One develops; princes and monarchs, which through the One adjust the empire: these are all effects of the One.

Were the heavens not thus clear they would be liable to rend; were the earth not thus reposeful, it would be liable to frothiness; were the gods not thus spiritual, they would be liable to imbecility; were space not thus full, it would be liable to exhaustion; were that which has form not thus developed, it would be liable to annihilation; were princes and monarchs not thus regulated, their dignities and honors would be liable to a downfall.

Hence humility is the root of honor: lowliness the foundation of loftiness. It is on this account that princes and monarchs style themselves "kithless," "friendless," "unworthies." Do they not thus acknowledge humility as their root?

The enumeration of the parts of a carriage do not make a carriage.

Desire neither the polish of the gem, nor the roughness of the stone.

Comment

When the senses rule they become vehicles of death and deceit. The emotions when uncontrolled, impart their color to every conclusion; when the desires are unregulated they compel the reason to think that their wishes are without blame, so that, until he has risen above sensation and desire, and can view himself as a being apart, man is unable to discriminate the true from the false and is liable to destruction. Until he rests in the undivided harmony of his spirit, and knows that pleasure and pain exist only in his *phenomenal* self, without any counterpart in his real life, man regards virtue and vice with blurred eyes, but "if thine eye be single, thy whole body is full of light." A truth-seeker must be selfless or he will fail in his search, an eye to personal results will vitiate his every inference and cause him to mistake parts of the carriage for the whole. Seek, therefore, THE ONE alone, and do not be drawn aside by desire, whether desire for the beauty of the gem or the roughness of the stone. Be identified with the spirit, not with the form. "Trust in the Lord with all thine heart, and lean not upon thine own understanding." (Prov. iii, 5) *Humility is the root of honor, lowliness the foundation of loftiness.*

CHAPTER 40

The movements of the Tao are cyclical; the sufficiency of the Tao is latency.[1]

All that is,[2] exists in being, being in non-being.[3]

Comment

"So is the kingdom of God, as if a man should cast seed upon the earth; and should sleep and rise night and day, and the seed should spring up and grow, he knoweth not how. The earth beareth fruit of herself; first the blade, then the ear, then the full grain in the ear." (Mark iv, 26-28) "The kingdom of heaven is like unto a grain of mustard seed, which a man took, and sowed in his field: which indeed is less than all seeds; but when it is grown, it is greater than the herbs, and becometh a tree, so that the birds of the heaven come and lodge in the branches thereof." (Matt xiii, 31, 32) "The kingdom of heaven is like unto leaven, which a woman took, and hid in three measures of meal, till it was all leavened." (Matt xiii, 33)

Notes

(1) Literally "weakness," the weakness of latent strength.
(2) Literally "heaven, earth, the myriad existences."
(3) The yet unformed ships exist in the forest trees.

CHAPTER 41

The true student hears of the Tao; he is diligent and practices it.

The average student hears of it; sometimes he appears to be attentive, then again he is inattentive.

The half hearted student hears of it; he loudly derides it. If it did not provoke ridicule it would not be worthy the name—Tao.

Again there are those whose only care is phraseology.

The brilliancy of the Tao is as obscurity; the advance of the Tao is as a retreat; the equality of the Tao is as inequality; the higher energy is as cosmic space; the greatest purity is as uncleanness; the widest virtue is as if insufficient;[1] established virtue is as if furtive; the truest essence is as imperfection; the most perfect square is cornerless; the largest vessel is last completed; the loudest sound has fewest tones; the grandest conception is formless.

The Tao is concealed and nameless, yet it is the Tao alone which excels in imparting and completing.

Comment

Of Himself the great Master said: "The foxes have holes and the birds of the heaven have nests; but the Son of man hath not where to lay his head." (Luke ix, 58) Of those who would be his disciples the same Master said: "He that loveth father or mother more than me is not worthy of me; and he that loveth son or daughter more than me is not worthy of me. And he that doth not take his cross and follow after me is not worthy of me." (Matt x, 37, 38) In the *Bhagavad Gita* the qualifications for discipleship are described as "Unattachment, absence of self-identification with son, wife or home, and constant balance of mind in wished-for and unwished-for events." "For narrow is the gate, and straitened the way, that leadeth unto life, and few are they that find it." (Matt. vii, 14) No wonder that when "the half hearted" hear of it, they loudly deride it. It means obscurity, retreat, self-repression, crucifixion, until the flesh rebels and cries out in bitterness, only to find its wail unheeded. There is nothing here to attract any but those who are indifferent to objects of sense. *Established virtue is as if furtive.* The square which is most complete is without parts, it has no corners; in the words of Paul, *the true student is* "as unknown, and yet well known; as dying, and behold, we live; as chastened, and not killed; as sorrowful, yet always rejoicing; as poor, yet making many rich; as having nothing, and yet possessing all things"; (II Cor. vi, 9, 10) for though *concealed and nameless, yet it is the Tao alone which excels in imparting and completing.*

Note

(1) The "Virtue" of this chapter is the "Energy" of chap. 38 and elsewhere.

CHAPTER 42

The Tao produced One. The One produced two; the two produced three;[1] the three produced all things.

Everything is permeated by the yin and the yang and vivified by the immaterial breath.[2]

That which men hate is to be kithless, friendless and considered unworthy, but princes and dukes thus style themselves.[3] From this it would appear that advantages are disadvantageous, and disadvantages are advantageous.

I teach that which others have taught.

The violent and the fierce do not live out their years.

I shall be chief among the teachers.[4]

Comment

The trinitarian conception is universal. It is seen in the three-fold character of cell growth—cell-enlargement, cell-specialization, cell-multiplication; in the triune process year by year of birth in spring, maturity in summer, decay in autumn; it is seen in the body, soul and spirit of which man is composed; and in the father, mother, offspring of the completed family life. As Zoroaster has said: "The number 3 reigns throughout the universe, and the Monad is its principle." It is natural therefore that Lao-tzu should give it a prominent position in his philosophy; equally natural that he should proceed without a break from the trinitarian process of creation to humility. For not only is the Trinity everywhere, but everywhere it is a sacrificing Trinity. The mineral kingdom gives its life for the vegetable, the vegetable for the anmal, while the mineral and the vegetable are helped toward the realization of their being by the expenditure of man's strength. So also in the Bible the Father yields the Son, the Son does not please himself (Rom. xv, 3), and the Spirit bears witness not to Himself, but to the other two persons of the Trinity. Self-sacrifice is the root of life. Who seeks loses; who loses finds. By this we perceive the advantages of the disadvantageous, and the disadvantages of the advantageous.

Notes

(1) Georg von der Gablentz observes that rendered literally this should read:

(Tao)+1+2+3=7. See Dr. Edkins' illuminative historical notes in *The China Review*, vol. 13, p. 16. Universal Genesis starts from the One, breaks into Three, then Five, and finally culminates in Seven, to return into Four, Three, and One. Cf. *The Secret Doctrine*, ii, 170, 658. See also iii, 397 et al.

(2) In an essay on Taoism published in the first volume of the *China Review*, Chalmers gives the following: "There is a Trinity observable in all the manifestations of Tao, corresponding to the three principal senses in man, hearing, seeing, and feeling, and to sound, color and form, in the external world. The terms of this trinity are generally in Chinese, *Yin, Yang* and *Hwo-hi*. The *Hwo-hi*—the harmonious Breath or Spirit—is held by Lao-tze to be present in nature intermediate between the *yin* and *yang;* which you must know, denotes in Chinese the two members of 'an inevitable dualism which bisects nature.' (Emerson) Heaven and Earth, for instance, are a duality, the greatest duality of which we have any cognizance, but there is an intermediate Breath—we may call it a Spirit,—shadowed forth in the spiritual nature of man, which constitutes the third term. Thus while the Confucianists, following the *Yih-king*, rest in dualism, and materialism, the Taoist, though denying an eternal, personal God, is a sort of Trinitarian, and the third member of his trinity is Spirit, personal or impersonal. No numerical character belongs to Tao, however, for Tao is *chaotic;* when the mind approaches that, all things seem to be blended in *unity* and it remains utterly inscrutable."

In the same essay we find the following quotation describing the Pythagorean theory of numbers:

"Unity is a male monad, begetting after the manner of a parent all the rest of the numbers. Secondly, the *duad* is a female number, and the same also is by arithmeticians called even. Thirdly, the *triad* is a male number. This also has been classified by arithmeticians under the denomination uneven. And in addition to all these is the *tetrad,* a female number, and the same also is called even, because it is female. Therefore all the numbers that have been derived from the genus are four; but number is the indefinite genus, from which was constituted according to them, the perfect number, namely the decade. For one, two, three, four become ten if its proper denomination be preserved essentially for each of the numbers. Pythagoras affirmed this to be a sacred quaternion source of everlasting nature, having, as it were, roots in itself; and that from this number all the numbers receive that originating principle. For eleven, and twelve, and the rest partake of the origin of existence from ten. Of this decade, the perfect number, there are termed four divisions, namely monad, square and cube. And the connections and blendings of these are performed, according to nature, for the generation of growth completing the productive number. For when the square is multiplied into itself, a biquadratic is the result. But when the square is multiplied into the cube, the result is the product of a square and cube; and when the cube is multiplied into the cube, the product of two cubes is the result. So that all the numbers from which the production of existing (numbers) arises is seven, namely monad, number, square, cube, biquadratic, quadratic cube, cubo-cube." *Hippolytus,* (Ante-Nicene Christian Library, vol. 6, p. 32.)

The above quotation would be perfectly intelligible to any Chinese scholar without explanations. Indeed it would be difficult to convince him that it had not been taken from his own writings.

(3) Indicating that any virtue they possess lies in the unsearchable realms of the infinite rather than on the objective plane of existence. See ch. 39.

(4) The advantages of weakness had been taught before Lao-tzu, but not the danger of self-assertiveness. It is on his insistence on this that Lao-tzu bases his claim to be a leader of the leaders. See chaps. 9, 29, 30, 73, 76.

CHAPTER 43

The world's weakest drives the world's strongest.
The indiscernible penetrates where there are no crevices.[1]

From this I perceive the advantages of non-action.[2]
Few indeed in the world realize the instructions of the silence, or the benefits of inaction.[3]

Comment

Those who have heard the voice which speaks in the silence, and have learned the benefits of non-action know that no armour is so safe a panoply as the shield of weakness, even according to that strange word of the Apostle Peter, "Forasmuch then as Christ suffered in the flesh, ARM yourselves also with the same mind." (I Peter iv, 1) The Christ conquered on the cross; His crown of thorns is a crown of crowns, and my greatest strength lies in my power to divest myself of self. Though indiscernible this power "penetrates where there are no crevices."

Notes

(1) "Without and within all beings, immovable and also movable; by reason of His subtlety imperceptible; at hand and far away is That."—*Bhagavad Gita.*

"For wisdom is more moving than any motion; she passeth and goeth through all things by reason of her pureness."—*Wisdom of Solomon,* vii, 24.

(2) As the indiscernible meets with no obstacles, so the power of non-action is irresistible.

(3) Chinese history supplies a severe, if somewhat crude example, of the doctrine of inaction. It is stated that when Ju-shih-ki (Tang dynasty, A.D. 618-905) was on the eve of accepting an official position, his uncle called him and said that he felt ill at ease respecting him. "What will you do, Nephew." he asked, "if some one strikes you?" "Receive the blow in meekness," was the reply. "If you are reviled, what then?" "I shall be silent." "What if you are spat upon?" "I shall wipe away the spittle." *"In doing that,"* answered his uncle, *"you may be showing resentment to the spitter, and that would be a wrong."*

CHAPTER 44

Fame or life, which is dearer? Life or wealth, which is more? Gain or loss, which is worse?

Excessive love implies excessive outlay. Immoderate accumulation implies heavy loss.[1]

Who knows contentment meets no shame. Who knows when to stop incurs no danger. Such long endure.

Comment

We possess nothing more valuable than our ideals, but the only ideal which is not immoderate is that ideal content which is content with nothing for self; to stop short of this is to linger where danger lurks. Mystics of all ages, irrespective of their religious profession have realized this. A few paragraphs from a Spanish Catholic of the sixteenth century—Saint Jean de la Croix—will illustrate Lao-tzu's thought:

"To enjoy the taste of all things, have no taste for anything,

"To know all things, learn to know nothing.

"To possess all things, resolve to possess nothing.

"To be all things, be willing to be nothing.

"To get to where you have no taste for anything, go through whatever experiences you have no taste for.

"To learn to know nothing, go whither you are ignorant.

"To reach what you possess not, go whithersoever you own nothing.

"To be what you are not, experience what you are not.

"When you stop at anything, you cease to open yourself to the All.

"For to come to the All, you must give up the All.

"And if you should attain to owning the All, you must own it, desiring Nothing."[2]

With this compare the saying by Lu Hui-neng, the sixth and last Chinese Buddhist Patriarch: "To be able to separate one's self from all affections is the pith of tranquillity."

Notes

(1) "Every excess causes a defect; every defect an excess."
Emerson's Essay on Compensation.

(2) Quoted in *The Varieties of Religious Experiences*
(Gifford Lectures, 1901-1902) by William James, p. 306.

CHAPTER 45

The greatest attainment is as though incomplete; but its utility remains unimpaired.

The greatest fulness is as a void; but its utility is inexhaustible.

The greatest uprightness is as crookedness; the greatest cleverness as clumsiness; the greatest eloquence as reticence.

Motion overcomes cold; stillness conquers heat. Purity and stillness are the world's standards.[1]

Comment

Read Paul's description of the work of the great Master of humility—the Lord Jesus. "Who, being in the form of God, counted it not a prize to be on an equality with God, but emptied Himself, taking the form of a servant, being made in the likeness of men; and being found in fashion as a man, He humbled Himself, becoming obedient even unto death, yea, the death of the cross." (Phil. ii, 6-8) His "greatest attainment" was His self-annihilation. "Wherefore also God highly exalted Him, and gave Him the name which is above every name." (Phil. ii, 9) Hear Paul once more on the same theme: "In Him dwelleth all the fulness of the Godhead bodily." (Col. ii, 9) But how does the Christ describe Himself? "I am meek and lowly of heart." (Matt. xii, 29) *The greatest fulness is as a void, but its utility is inexhaustible.*" Paul writes of Jesus the Christ, as He "Who is the image of the invisible God, the first-born of all creation," (Col. i, 15) but to His disciples Jesus said, "I am in the midst of you as he that serveth" (Luke xxii, 27) and later, as if to further impress this upon them, He washed their feet. The stillness of His heart conquered the heat of their passions; it is the movings of His love which is overcoming the cold isolations, dividing the different peoples. In the purity and stillness of His inner being He illustrates Nature's profoundest secret. "Nature," says Emerson, "will not have us fret and fume. She does

not like our benevolence, our learning, much better than she likes our frauds and wars. When we come out of the caucus, or the bank, or the Abolition convention or the Temperance meeting, or the Transcendental Club into the fields and woods, she says to us, 'So hot? my little sir.' "
Purity and stillness are the world's standards.

Notes

(1) Ho-shang-kung, with a fine perception of the greatness inseparable from goodness, remarks: "Heaven and earth yield to the man who is pure and still."

"Purity and stillness" are according to Wu-ch'eng attributes of non-action (or non-attachment).

CHAPTER 46

When the empire is controlled by the Tao, riding horses are employed in agriculture; when the empire is without Tao, war horses are in every open space.[1]

There is no sin greater than covetousness; no calamity greater than discontent; no fault greater than acquisitiveness.

Who therefore knows the contentment of content possesses unchanging content.

Comment

"Everywhere THAT has hands and feet, everywhere eyes, head, mouths; all-hearing, He dwelleth in the world, enveloping all," sang the ancient Indian poet. "The eyes of all wait upon Thee; and thou givest them their meat in due season," chanted the Hebrew Psalmist. Yet the world is devastated continually, and plunged into the miseries of war by man's covetousness. What would become of the race if the ALL-FATHER, like his children, were acquisitive—moved by desires for the personal self? How is the empire to be freed from that which is not-TAO—covetousness— and brought under the control of the TAO so that all shall enjoy the "unchanging content?" Chu-hsi, the great Confucian commentator, shall supply the answer:

"Heaven and man are not properly two, and man is separate from heaven only by having this body. Of their seeing and hearing, their thinking and revolving, their moving and acting, men all say, *It is from* Me." Every one thus brings out his SELF, and his smallness becomes known. But let the body be taken away, and all would be heaven. How can the body be taken away? Simply by subduing and removing that self-having of the *ego*. This is the taking it away.

Note

(1) "In the former case says Han Fei Tzu, there will be no work for soldiers. In the latter, lice will swarm in the armour, and swallows build their nests in the tents—of soldiers who return no more,"—*Remains of Lao Tzu.*

CHAPTER 47

The world may be known without going out of doors.

The heavenly way (Tao) may be seen without looking through the window.[1]

The further one goes the less one knows.

Hence the Holy Man arrives without traveling;[2] names without looking; accomplishes without action.[3]

Comment

The knowledge of the Sage is intuitive. He requires only to concentrate his attention on a subject to understand it. All men have intuitions, certain facts of which they are convinced without having reasoned on them, but most are guided by impulse, their motives arise in that which is without, instead of from what is within. The man who is dependent on reason, like the blind man who relies on touch, is liable to deception. *The further he goes the less he knows.* The *Heavenly Way* is only perceptible to the inner eye. "If therefore thine eye be single, thy whole body shall be full of light." *Hence the Sage arrives without traveling.* So also the Upanishads: "Though sitting still, he walks far; though lying down he goes everywhere." Says Alipili: "If that which thou seekest thou findest not within thee thou wilt never find it without thee."

"Truth is within ourselves; it takes no rise
From outward things, whate'er you may believe."

By concentration on this inner universe, by meditation on the Higher Self, by unselfish obedience to the holy vision, *the world may be known without going out of doors.* The unselfish, who are devoid of self-seeking, who subordinate the finite to the Universal Will, may follow this Divinity within wherever it leads. "If ye abide in my word, then are ye truly my disciples; and ye shall know the truth, and the truth shall make you free." (John viii, 32) The pure in heart, or the single-minded "see God."

Notes

(1) Su-cheh writes, "Spirit is universal, knowing nothing of either near or far, ancient or modern. It is thus that the Sage knows everything without going from the door, or looking through the window. Men of the present day are limited by matter, the spirit within them is limited by ears and eyes, thus they are thrown into confusion be-sires and by their bodies; thus mountains and rivers become barriers; they know nothing excepting what their eyes see, or their ears hear, and in this way even such trifles as doors and windows obstruct them. Are you not aware that the Sage having recovered his original nature is satisfied? Why desire to go abroad to search? The farther you go the less you will know." See *The Voice of the Silence*.

Wang-pi says: "All things have one ancestry; all roads meet at one point; all thought leads to the same conclusion; all religions point to the same goal."

(2) I.e. he knows intuitively and does not require to go over each point step by step.

(3) Comp. Deut. xxx, 12-14, Rom. x, 6-8.

CHAPTER 48

The pursuit of study brings daily increase; the pursuit of Tao daily decrease; decrease upon decrease, until non-action is reached, whence all action proceeds.[1]

Only continued non-concern will win the Empire; where there is concern there is an insufficiency for the task.

Comment

As mere outwardness retreats the true inwardness is discerned. Beware lest intellectual evolution become spiritual devolution. God has chosen "the things that are not, that He might bring to naught the things that are." *Study brings daily increase, the Tao daily decrease, until nonaction is reached.* The force with which men of violence seize the Kingdom of God is not the self-assertion of the passions, but that mystic force which does violence to the lower nature, plucks out the right eye, or cuts off the right foot. This philosophy is not concerned lest it suffer wrong, or be defrauded of right, knowing that *only continued nonconcern will win the Empire.*

"Surely," says Thomas à Kempis, "an humble husbandman that serveth God is better than a proud philosopher who, neglecting himself, is occupied in studying the course of the heavens."

Note

(1) Students will find illumination on this chapter in the earlier pages of *The Voice of the Silence.*

CHAPTER 49

The Holy Man is not inflexible, he plans according to the needs of the people.

I would return good for good. I would also return good for evil.[1] Thus goodness operates (or "thus all become good").

I would return trust for trust. I would also return trust for suspicion. Thus trust operates (or "thus all become trustworthy").

The Holy Man as he dwells in the world is very apprehensive concerning it, blending his heart with the whole.[2] Most men plan for themselves.[3] The Holy Man treats every one as a child.[4]

Comment

The Sage, calm and passionless, without regrets, without desires, having risen above all that is separative, adapts himself to the needs of mankind as water to the shape of the vessel into which it is poured. Knowing that, as a Japanese proverb expresses it, pleasure is the seed of pain, pain is the seed of pleasure *(raku wa ku no tané; ku wa raku no tané)*, he treats all men, the good and the bad, the sincere and the insincere, with equal benevolence. Alfred Sutro records of Maeterlinck that he regarded the humble, the foolish, the saint, the sinner, with the same love and almost the same admiration. "Nothing is contemptible in this world but scorn." "He maketh his sun to rise on the evil and the good, and sendeth rain on the just and the unjust." (Matt. v, 45)

Notes

(1) Cf. ch. 63. "The man who returns good for evil is as a tree which renders its shade and its fruit even to those who cast stones at it."—Persian Proverb.

(2) "In the world good and evil, trustworthiness and hy-

pocrisy arise from too much emphasis being placed on the personality. In this way mutual recriminations and injuries arise, without any standard whereby they may be decided. The Sage, apprehensive concerning these, blends his heart with the whole, and treats all, the good and the bad, the trustworthy and the hypocrite alike."—*Su-cheh*. Cf. *The Path of Discipleship,* by Annie Besant.

(3) Literally "direct their thoughts to their own ears and eyes." My rendering is supported by such commentators as Wang-pi and Ho-shang-kung. The passage has been usually modeled according to the teachings of *The Doctrine of The Mean,* and made to say that all the people turned their eyes toward the Sage.

(4) He makes no distinctions but treats all with equal impartiality. The same note was struck by the *Mahabharata.* "There is no distinction of castes; the whole world is created by God."

"The friend, or the enemy, is merely the ascription of the desire nature to certain patent facts, and varies with the attitude of the mind."—*Studies in The Bhagavad Gita,* by The Dreamer (*The Yoga of Discrimination*).

CHAPTER 50

Birth is an exit; death an entrance.[1]

Three in ten are ways of life; three in ten are ways of death; three in ten also of those who live move into the realm of death.[2] Why is this? Because of their excessive strivings after life.[3] It has been said that he who thoroughly understands how to care for his life will not need to shun the rhinoceros or the tiger; he need not fear weapons even in the midst of a battle. The rhinoceros finds no place into which to thrust its horn; the tiger no place into which to fix its claws; nor the sword a place into which to flesh its point. Why is this? Because such an one is not moved by the thought of death.[4]

Comment

"So dear to heav'n is saintly chastity,
That when a soul is found sincerely so,
A thousand liveried angels lackey her,
Driving far off each thing of sin and guilt,
And in clear dream, and solemn vision,
Tell her of things that no gross ear can hear,
Till oft converse with heav'nly habitants
Begin to cast a beam on th' outward shape,
The unpolluted temple of the mind,
And turns it by degrees to the soul's essence,
Till all be made immortal."

—Milton's *Comus*

"When all desires that dwell in the heart cease, then the mortal becomes immortal, and obtains Brahman."

—Upanishads

Notes

(1) "We begin our life surrounded by the Karma of our former existences; as we have acted during life so we leave

113

it to enter another existence."—Thos. Kingsmill, *loc. cit.*

A Chinese commentator supplies the following: "When the passions come out from a man, and he within is calm, he lives: when they enter and so lead to action, he dies."

(2) The text is enigmatical. Scholars are not agreed as to whether it should read "Three in ten" or "Thirteen." I have tried to faithfully represent the text, but see *The Secret Doctrine,* vol. i, pp. 401-403: $2 \times 6 + 1 = 13$; also, vol. ii, 440.

(3) Prof. Legge describes the first three as "those who eschewed all things, both internal and external, tending to injure health"; The second three as "those who pursued courses likely to cause disease and shorten life; the third would be those who thought that by mysterious and abnormal courses they could prolong life, but only injured it. Those three classes being thus disposed of, there remains only one in ten rightly using the Tao, and he is spoken of in the next paragraph."

(4) Mencius quotes the philosopher Tsang as saying "If, on self-examination, I find that I am not upright, shall I not be in fear even of a poor man in his loose garments of hair cloth? If, on self-examination, I find that I am upright, I will go forward against thousands and tens of thousands."

Says Chuang-tzu: "The Sage," answered Wang-i, "is a spiritual being. If the ocean were scorched up he would not feel hot. If all the rivers were frozen hard he would not feel cold."

CHAPTER 51

What the Tao produces and its energy[1] nourishes, nature forms and natural forces establish. On this account there is nothing that does not honor the Tao and reverence its energy. This honor and reverence are spontaneous, not the result of a mandate.

So the Tao produces. Its energy nourishes, increases, feeds, establishes, matures, controls, broods over. It produces, but keeps nothing for itself; acts, but does not depend on its action; increases, but does not insist on having its own way. This indeed is the mystery of energy.[2]

Comment

> "The lark
> Soars up and up, shivering for very joy;
> Afar the ocean sleeps; white fishing gulls
> Flit where the strand is purple with its tribe
> Of nested limpets; subject creatures seek
> Their loves in wood and plane—and God renews
> His common rapture."

Professor Drummond expresses the innerness of this chapter when he writes—"Are we quite sure, that what we call a physical world, is, after all a physical world? . . . The very term 'natural world,' we are told, is a misnomer; that the world is a spiritual world, merely employing 'matter' for its manifestation." "Raise the stone and there thou shalt find me, cleave the wood and there am I." *Sayings of our Lord.* (Logion v.)

Notes

(1) The word rendered "energy" is again the *Teh* of chap. 38. "That which below produces the grain, and above becomes the stars, that which circulates through heaven and

earth, is called the Divine Energy."—*Kuan-tzu.* Wu-ch'eng in his commentary refuses to distinguish between the Tao and its energy. Cf. Eph. iv, 6.

(2) Translated by Dr. Edkins "secret energy." The original is "secret or profound Teh." Comp. the conclusion of chap. 2.

See "A Vision of Beginnings," The *Theosophical Review,* vol. 30, p. 125.

CHAPTER 52

Everything has its origin in the mother of all under heaven.[1]

To know the mother the child must be perceived; the child being born the qualities of the mother must be maintained, to the end of life there will be then no peril.[2]

Close the doors of the senses, and the whole of life will be without care; open them, attend to the affairs of life and to the end deliverance will be impossible.[3]

Perceive the germ, that is enlightenment.[4]

Maintain weakness, that is stability.

Employ the light; revert to this enlightenment; no calamity will then be bequeathed to the body.[5]

This is indeed to practice the unalterable.[6]

Comment

Those who live the life of the body die, but for those who live the life of soul

> "There is no death! The stars go down
> To rise upon some other shore,
> And bright in heaven's jeweled crown
> They shine for evermore."

Notes

(1) In all mythologies the male stands for the Unmanifest, the female for the manifested—the womb which gave birth to creation. See Isis, and the goddess Moot, the Mother, of Egypt, the Sephira of the Kabalists; Aditi of the Hindus; Sophia of the Gnostics; Wisdom in the Proverbs of Solomon. In all theogonies we find the symbol of the egg, the ovum of the mystic mother. In Christendom it survives in the "Easter Egg."

(2) Separation is necessary for growth, but safety lies in the preservation of the consciousness of non-separateness.

(3) The text may be illustrated by a parable from Chuang-tzu: "There was once a man who was afraid of his own shadow, and had a strong dislike to his own footprints. So he tried to escape from both; but the quicker he ran the more footprints he made, and fast as he went his shadow kept up with him. He thought he was going too slowly, so he ran faster and faster without stopping, until his strength gave out and he fell dead. He did not know that if he strayed in a shady place his shadow would have disappeared, and that if he had only remained quiet and motionless he would not have made any footprints. Stupid fellow that he was."—*Chuang-tzu* by Balfour.

(4) "Injuries spring from desires, though small in the beginning they swell to great dimensions. Now to know that the small will become great, and to exclude it, that may be said to be enlightenment."—*Su-cheh*.

(5) Bodily vigor, like mental purity, depends on what the mind relates itself to.

(6) Compare chaps. 16 and 55.

CHAPTER 53

When knowledge compels me to practice the supreme Tao, the danger lies in putting it into action.[1]

The supreme Tao is a vast plain, yet the people prefer bypaths. The palace is magnificent, but the fields are full of weeds; the granaries are empty, but elegant clothes are worn; sharp two-edged swords are carried, fastidiousness in eating and drinking is displayed, many useless things are amassed—this is robbery and swaggering.[2]

This is not the Tao![3]

Comment

The true life of the soul is realized as it exercises its power apart from the senses. Until reborn into the spiritual the senses are blind to the beautiful, or simplicity without superfluity. Man, not realizing this, prefers the bypaths in the lowlands of the physical. These, says Lao-tzu, are not the TAO. To comprehend THAT one must, in the language of Michael de Molinos, know that the center of the kingdom of God is the soul; this must be kept quiet, unoccupied, peaceful, free from fault (personal), inclinations and desires.

Notes

(1) Translators differ widely.

(2) If, says Han Fei Tzu as rendered by Giles in his *Remains of Lao Tzu,* "If accumulation of property prevail in the State, the ignorant masses will naturally take to chicanery in imitation of their betters, and thieving will come into vogue. The lower classes respond to the higher precisely as the lesser musical instruments of a band follow the leading instruments."

A lesson for modern times. Extravagance now-a-days is common, where there should be economy, economy is practiced where there should be extravagance. There is much extravagance in the glory and swagger of war, and too much economy in the impartation of the economic science and the fine arts.

(3) The Tao is Simplicity. *vide* chap. 32.

CHAPTER 54

Who plants well will not have his work uprooted; who embraces well will not lose what he holds; the offerings of his sons and grandsons will never end.[1]

Who thus regulates himself has virtue which is genuine; who thus regulates his household has virtue which overflows; who thus regulates his neighborhood has virtue which excels; who thus regulates the state has virtue which abounds; who thus regulates the world has virtue[2] which is universal.

Therefore let every man prove himself; let each household, neighborhood, and state do the same; let the world also follow the same course.

How do I know that it must be thus with the world? By this same (which has been just said).

Comment

"The kingdom of God is within you." "Every plant which my heavenly Father planted not, shall be rooted up." "Let not your heart be troubled: ye believe in God, believe also in me. In my Father's house are many abiding places."

This was the teaching, and the daily experience of the Lord Jesus. Whoever roots his life on these levels will not only be never swept from off his feet but will become a regulative force, which will not cease at the stage called death. The offerings of his sons and grandsons will never end.

Notes

(1) "Where is that which is so planted that it cannot be uprooted, or so held that it cannot be torn away? Only the Sage knows the truth of spirit and the illusion of matter, so that he can give up the latter for the sake of the former. His virtue overflows, but indeed he establishes nothing, so

that what he establishes cannot be uprooted. Truly he grasps nothing, and so what he embraces cannot be taken from him. Will not his sons and his grandsons be able therefore to continue their sacrifices without ceasing?"—*Su-cheh*.

(2) "Virtue" (*teh*) is the same Chinese word as that translated "energy" in chaps. 38, 51, 55, etc.

CHAPTER 55

Who cherishes energy in abundance is comparable to an infant child. Poison insects will not sting him; fierce beasts will not seize him; birds of prey will not strike him.[1]

His bones are weak; his sinews pliable; his grip firm;[2] unconscious of sex, his virility is active[3]—the excellency of his physique. He may cry all day without becoming hoarse—this is the consummation of harmony.

Knowledge of harmony is called "The Unalterable;"[4] knowledge of the Unalterable is called "Illumination."

Increase of life is called infelicity, the resting of the mind in the vitality of form is called animality.

The corporeal begins to age as it nears its prime. This indeed is not the Tao. What is not the Tao soon ends.[5]

Comment

"The Great Man never loses his child's heart." says Mencius, and Lao-tzu in language which is both quaint and suggestive expands the same thought. The infant has neither the desire nor the ability to appreciate sensuous pleasure. It may cry all day and not become hoarse. It lacks that passionate vehemence which would produce exhaustion after a similar effort by an adult. Its innocence and its weakness are its strength. It receives no harm from poisonous insects, fierce beasts, or cruel birds—the lusts and passions of the animal man. Without prejudices, the infant seeks only that which is essential, "mother's milk," indifferent whether it comes from this woman, or from that. Its inner harmony is undisturbed. Its bodily organs are perfect; the years add nothing to them, but only develop their functions, but do not add to them. "Except ye turn and become as little

children, ye shall in no wise enter the kingdom of heaven."—
Matt. xviii, 3.

Says the *Bhagavad Gita*: "The contacts of the senses,
O son of Kunti, giving cold and heat, pleasure and pain,
they come and go, impermanent; endure them bravely, O
Bharata. The man whom these torment not, O chief of
men, balanced in pain and pleasure, steadfast, he is fitted
for immortality."—Ch. 2, 14-15. *He has escaped from that
which "is not the Tao."*

Notes

(1) Hsü-hui-hi explains this to mean that nature will
cease to be inimical to man when man ceases to injure Nature. Cf. chap. 50.

(2) "A curious anticipation of recent scientific investigation into the clinging power of new-born infants."—Maclagan.

(3) "Baby boys before emptying the bladder are frequently troubled with erections, which is here misinterpreted as
a symbol of vigor."—Carus.

(4) See conclusion of chap. 52. Also comp. chap. 16.

(5) The two concluding paragraphs express the opposite
of the eternal, or unalterable. The conclusion of this chapter is almost identical with that of chap. 30.

CHAPTER 56

Who knows does not speak; who speaks does not know.[1]

Close the doors of the senses; blunt the sharp; unravel the confused; harmonize the dazzling; become one with the all. This is the Mystery of Unity.[2] There will then neither be love nor hate; profit nor loss; favor nor disgrace. It follows that in the universe there is nothing nobler.[3]

Comment

"The profoundest truths of spiritual experience are those which are not intellectually ascertained but spiritually discerned, which are not taught to us but revealed in us; and these never can be adequately put into words. They defy definition; they transcend expression. The highest experiences even of earthly love and hope and joy cannot be translated into terms of common speech. As there is a life which can be expressed only in terms of music, and another which is expressible only in terms of art, so there is a life which is truly inexpressible. All that he who has obtained even a glimpse of this realm can hope to do is to afford a glimpse to others, by recalling a like experience in their life, 'comparing spiritual things with spiritual.' "—*Lyman Abbott.*

Notes

(1) "The moment a man can really do his work he becomes speechless about it."—*Sesame and Lilies,* by John Ruskin.

"But why should we expound our own views uncalled for? The danger of self-assertion is there."—*The Science of the Emotions* by Bhagavan Das.

(2) "Blunt your own sharp points and you will be able to unravel the confusion of others; soften your own glare, and you will be able to put yourself on a level with others;

then, when there is no difference between yourself and others, when you are one with the world, you will have attained to spiritual experiences which are inexpressible. Hence it is called the mystery of unity."—*Wu-ch'eng.* Cf. Matt. vii. 1-5.

(3) Chaps. 4 and 52.

CHAPTER 57

Rule the Empire with uprightness. The employment of the military is a strange device. The Empire is won by non-concern. How do I know this? Thus: The more superstitious restrictions in the land the poorer the people;[1] the more the people are concerned with the administration the more benighted the state and the clans;[2] the more craftiness is displayed the greater the number of novelties which arise. The more legislation there is the more thieves and robbers increase.

It is for these reasons that a sage has said[3]: "I do nothing, but the people spontaneously reform. I love tranquillity, and the people spontaneously become upright. I have no concerns, and the people naturally grow wealthy. I am without desire, and of their own free will the people revert to primitive simplicity."[4]

Comment

"Which of you by being anxious can add one cubit unto his stature?" The Kingdom of God is not won by anxiety. Self-assertion, desires to better clothe and feed the self, are "strange devices." Evil is not overthrown by resistance but by submission; it is not the passive quiet of the coward, nor the sullen stolidity of the slave, but the selfless service of the Christ, which disarms the enemy. When the left cheek is voluntarily submitted for a blow like that which stings the right, when the cloak is given to him who snatches the coat, when not only is the demand for the first mile granted, but the second also, and that from sheer goodwill toward the oppressor, evil becomes ashamed, it cannot understand such carelessness. *The Empire is won by non-concern.*

Notes

(1) Where weeds abound flowers are scarce.

(2) See chap. 36.

(3) There were Sages before Lao-tzu, and their teachings were his, but their names have been forgotten, and their works lost.

(4) "He who would have good government in his country must begin by putting his house in order, and to do that, he must begin by attending properly to his personal conduct."—*The Great Learning*. Comp. chap. 19.

CHAPTER 58

When the government is not in evidence[1] the people are honest and loyal.

When the government is meddlesome the people are in want.

Misery! Happiness lies by its side![2] Happiness! Misery lurks beneath. He who understands the end has progressed beyond limitations.

The regular becomes the irregular; the good becomes unpropitious. This has bewildered men from time immemorial!

Hence the Holy Man is a square which has not been cut, and whose corners have not been planed;[3] he is straightforward without being reckless, and bright without being dazzling.

Comment

The chapter proceeds from the outer to the inner, from that which is objective and manifest to that which is subjective and not so manifest. The evils of a meddlesome government are plain, they arise from too much emphasis being placed on externals rather than on principles. Less manifest to the "man on the street" is the trouble which arises from confusing happiness and misery, which are not separate but the reverse sides of the same shield. Jesus referred all his experiences, the success which attended his preaching, and the sorrow in which sin involved him, equally to the Father's will.

"Omnes! Omnes! Let others ignore what they may,
I make the poem of evil also, I commemorate that part also,
I am myself just as much evil as good, and my nation is—
    And I say there is in fact no evil
(Of if there is, I say it is just as important, to the land or
    to me as anything else)."

Thus the poet Walt Whitman, in his "Starting from Paumanok," confirms, in his own fashion, the teaching of our pre-Christian Chinese mystic. Robert Browning also sings the same theme in one of his later poems:

"Ask him—'Suppose the Gardener of Man's ground
    Plants for a purpose, side by side with good,
Evil—(and that he does so—look around!
    What does the field show?)—were it understood
That purposely the noxious plant was found
    Vexing the virtuous, poison close to food.
If, at first stealing forth of life in stalk
And leaflet-promise, quick his spud should balk
Evil from budding foliage, bearing fruit?
Such timely treatment of the offending root
Might strike the simple as wise husbandry,
But swift sure extirpation would scarce suit
Shrewder observers. Seed once sown thrives: why
Frustrate its product, miss the quality
Which sower binds himself to count upon?
Had seed fulfilled the destined purpose, gone
Unhindered up to harvest—what know I
But proof were gained that every growth of good
Sprang consequent on evil's neighborhood?' "

Notes

(1) Like the sun behind the clouds, felt but not seen.

(2) "Calamitas virtutis occasion." (Calamity is virtue's opportunity.)—*Seneca*.

(3) The Sage is four-square, perfect, not because he has become adjusted to the limitations of time and space, but because he has risen above these and is one with the invisible.

"The peace which comes of surrendering all likes and dislikes is possible only when the Triangle becoming Quaternary is inscribed in the Circle, when the Perfect Man—unifying his consciousness by indrawing the purified personality—so expands as to step beyond the limitations of the causal body and embrace the Logos—when the Divine Man, now a perfect square, recognizes Himself as a mode of expression of the Divine Life, a form of the Divine Consciousness, an organ of *Iswara* and an image and reflection of the true Self."—*Studies in the Bhagavad Gita* by The Dreamer, (*The Yoga of Discrimination*).

CHAPTER 59

For the regulation of mankind and the service of heaven nothing equals reserve power.[1] Reserve power means a speedy submission. Speedy submission implies a rich store of energy. A rich store of energy means the subjugation of everything. Everything being subdued none knows his limits. His limits being unknown his sovereign power is assured, having the root[2] of sovereignty which endures for long.

This may be described as a "deep taproot," and a "durable peduncle,"—the perpetual vitality and continued manifestation of the Tao.

Comment

The Tao, the eternal THAT is all powerful because It remains ever beyond the attraction to this or that. Therefore the Lord Jesus taught his disciples that the way to obtain all that is needful for earth is to seek *first* the kingdom of God and his righteousness.

Notes

(1) Literally "parsimoniousness"; "the harvest which must not be wasted."
(2) Literally "mother."

CHAPTER 60

Govern a great state as you would fry a small fish.

Employ the Tao to establish the Empire and the daemons will display no energy; not that they are devoid of energy, but that they will not use it to man's detriment; (further) not only will man suffer no hurt from the daemons but he will not be injured by the sages.

When neither harm, the attributes of the Tao blend and converge.[1]

Comment

Error cannot withstand truth. To practice the constant presence of God is the surest talisman against all evil. To him who dwells "in the secret place of the Most High" it is ever true that he knows neither the evil nor the plague. "No weapon that is formed against thee shall prosper." (*Vide* Psa., xci.)

Notes

(1) With one accord Lao-tzu's translators condemn this chapter as utterly unintelligible, it may therefore be as well to supply a paraphrase.

As a small fish stewing in the pan will be broken up if it be moved about too much, so will the Empire be fatally injured if its natural development be interfered with. The only safe course is to follow the Tao; That if employed for the regulation of mankind will make everyone a sage in due course in which case all will be safe from evil. The daemons could harm no one if there were not some affinity between them and the injured, and in like manner the sages can only benefit those who are akin with themselves. Lao-tzu in the text expresses this by saying that mankind will receive no hurt from the sages, that is to say they will receive positive good, for the absence of benefits is in itself an injury. When, in a word, the Tao is supreme, man receives neither positive harm from the spiritual forces which surround him, nor negative injury from the elders of his race who are ever ready to help all capable of receiving it. Cf. chap. 66.

"Attributes of the Tao" is represented in the Chinese by the character elsewhere translated "Energy."

CHAPTER 61

A great country is lowly. Everything under heaven blends with it. It is like the female, which at all times and in every place overcomes the male by her quietude. Than quietude there is nothing that is more lowly. Therefore a great state gains the smaller state by yielding; while the smaller state wins the greater by submission. In the one case lowliness gains adherents, in the other it procures favors.

For a strong state there is no safer ambition than to desire to gather men and care for them; and for the weaker state there is nothing better than the ambition to become an indispensable servant.

When each obtains what each desires the strongest should be the humblest.[1]

Comment

A passage from *The Varieties of Religious Experience*, by William James (p. 372) forms an excellent commentary on this section of Lao-tzu's writing: "Reenacted in human nature is the fable of the wind, the sun, and the traveler. The sexes embody the discrepancy. The woman loves the man the more admiringly the stormier he shows himself, and the world deifies its rulers the more for being wilful and unaccountable. But the woman in turn subjugates the man by the mystery of gentleness in beauty, and the saint has always charmed the world by something similar. Mankind is susceptible and suggestible in opposite directions, and the rivalry of influences is unsleeping."

Notes

(1) Dr. Carus has the following note to this chapter: "States in a federative empire, such as was the Chinese empire in the days of Lao-Tsze, grow powerful when they serve

the common interests of the whole nation. It would be as impossible for great rivers to flow in high mountains as for great states not to be subservient to the universal needs of the people. Streams become naturally great when they flow in the lowlands where they will receive all the other rivers as tributaries. The largest states are not always the greatest states. A state acquires and retains the leadership not by oppressing the other states, but by humbly serving them, by flowing lower than they. This truth has been preached by Christ when he said: 'Whosoever will be great among you, let him be your minister; and whosoever will be chief among you, let him be your servant.' An instance in the history of China that illustrates Lao-Tsze's doctrine, which at first sight appears as paradoxical as all his other teachings, is the ascendancy of the House of Cho, which under the humble but courageous Wu Wang succeeded the Shang dynasty, whose last emperor, Chow Sin (1122 B.C.) received the posthumous title Show, the abandoned tyrant. Other instances in history are the rise of Athens in Greece and of Prussia in Germany. Athens' ascendancy began when, in patriotic self-sacrifice, it served the cause of Greece, namely, of all the Greek states; and its decay set in with the oppression of the Athenian confederates, i.e. when Athens ceased to serve and began to use the resources of the Ionian confederacy for its own home interests."—*Lao-Tsze's Tao-Teh-King,* by Paul Carus, pp. 313, 314.

CHAPTER 62

The Tao has of all things the most honored place.[1]

It is the good man's treasure, and that which protects the bad man.

Its excellent words may be displayed before all. Its noble deeds assist all men.

Why should a man be cast aside because he is bad?[2]

Hence when the sovereign has been enthroned, and the chief ministers have been appointed, though one escorted by a team of horses, present the jade symbol of office, it would not equal the stilling of the heart, and entering this Tao.

What is the reason that this Tao has been held in such esteem from the beginning? May we not say that it is because those who seek receive, and those who are guilty escape by its (help)?[3] Hence it becomes the most valued thing under heaven.[4]

Comment

The noumenal is the real, the phenomenal, the reflection, and the wise man seeks the former rather than the latter. Earth's fairest pageantries are insignificant compared with That—her costliest gifts as dust compared with That. Only as man harmonizes with That can he escape the nemesis of guilt, a harmony which is possible because God and man are identical, differing only as the infinite differs from the finite; the impure or dfferentiated from the pure or undifferentiated. Jesus is at once a door through which God enters the generations of sin, and through which sinners pass into the realms of the eternal.

Notes

(1) This is the rendering of Dr. James Legge.
(2) "To merely regard the external appearance of things

is like standing outside the hall door, the TAO is within, and That is the most honorable. Men fail to perceive that all things possess It. However, the man of virtue knows that the Tao is his, and hence it is said to be 'the good man's treasure.' But the foolish and ignorant man also possesses the Tao, otherwise he would not be able to endure. Hence it is said to be 'the bad man's guardian.' Though men wander far from the Tao, the Tao never departs far from men."—*Su-cheh.*

(3) This is the only place in the *Tao-teh-king* where the idea of guilt occurs. The notion is Buddhistic, rather than Taoistic or Confucian.

(4) "Men, alas, will not seek for the root of truth. It is within themselves. If they sought it they would find it. The Tao has neither merit nor demerit, but men unfortunately do not understand this. If they did they would escape the defilement of sin."—*Su-cheh.*

"The Tao (path) may not be left for an instant. If it could be left it would not be the Tao (path)."—*The Doctrine of the Mean.*

CHAPTER 63

Practice non-action.[1] Be concerned with non-concern.[2] Taste the flavorless. Account the small as great, and the few as many.[3] For hatred return perfection.[4]

Manipulate difficulties while they are easy. Take in hand great things while they are insignificant. Every difficult thing in the world had its origin in what was at first easy. Every great thing in the world was once insignificant. Therefore the Holy Man makes no distinctions and thus he is able to accomplish that which is great.[5]

Small faith can be placed in promises lightly made.[6]

The easier a matter is reckoned the more difficult it proves at the last; for this reason the Holy Man sees difficulties in everything, and therefore he encounters no difficulties.

Comment

The man who has tasted the flavor of the flavorless, in which all flavors are concealed, is detached and free; he regards everything as alike great and alike small; as equally difficult and equally easy; neither careless nor indifferent; undertaking the most difficult tasks with ease, yet not overlooking the difficulties involved in the easiest affairs, he completes the greatest without difficulty. Living in the eternal, he neither cleaves to this, nor swerves from that.

This is the ideal life!

"What you do not wish others to do unto you, do not do unto them," said Confucius. Of Buddha it is recorded that he said, "A man who foolishly does me wrong I will return to him the protection of my ungrudging love; the more evil comes from him, the more good shall go from me." "He who beareth no ill-will to any being, friendly and compassionate, without attachment and egoism, balanced in pleasure and pain, and forgiving, ever content, harmonious, with the self controlled, resolute, with Manas and Buddhi dedicated to Me, he, My devotee, is dear to Me," was one of Krishna's instructions to Arjuna. In an earlier section Lao-tzu wrote "I would return good for good. I would also return good for evil." In a similar spirit Jesus said to his disciples "Resist not him that is evil; but whosoever smiteth thee on thy right cheek, return to him the other also. Love your enemies, and pray for them that persecute you."

The same commands confront us, no matter to what religious teacher we turn. By each we are told to rise above the love which is personal, whose shadow is hate, to the love which is universal, in which there is no room for hate; then we are bid rise still higher to the Love which is impersonal, which, because it identifies itself with All, is a segment of the circle which unites the divinity of man with the humanity of God, which sees greatness in the smallest and knows no distinctions. It promises nothing without a full sense of its responsibility. It is prepared for every difficulty, therefore It is able to meet hatred and misrepresentation with Perfection.

Notes

(1) *vide* Manual iv. p. 65 *et seq.*

(2) Cf, I Pet. v. 7, Matt. vi, 25-34.

(3) Because there is "nothing either great or small."

(4) "For hatred return perfection," i. e. avoid any emotion which will create in fellow-beings "any of the emotions on the side of hate and vice." Be "as gold that melts and becomes the purer the more it is exposed to the fire." "Perfection" is another rendering of the Chinese character elsewhere translated "energy." It includes all the attributes of the Tao.

(5) He recognizes no distinctions such as important and unimportant. The text might be rendered "Therefore the Holy Man does not attempt great things, and on that account he is able to accomplish the greatest."

(6) "The Master said 'He who speaks without modesty will find it difficult to make his words good.' "—Confucian *Analects*, xiv, 21.

CHAPTER 64

Whatever is at rest can easily be taken in hand; while yet no omens have appeared plans can be easily formed.

What is brittle is easily broken; what is minute is easily scattered.

Act before necessity arises; regulate before disorder commences.[1]

The trunk that can scarcely be embraced sprang from a tiny shoot; the tower that is nine stories high was raised from a mound of earth; the journey of a thousand li[2] commenced when the foot was placed on the ground.[3]

Who makes, mars; who grasps, loses.[4]

The Holy Man practices non-action, hence he never injures; he never grasps, hence he never loses. The majority are too eager for results in attending to their affairs, and spoil everything. There would be no such failures were they as cautious at the end as at the beginning.[5]

Hence the Holy Man desires passionlessness;[6] he does not prize articles that are rare; he studies to be unlearned;[7] he reverts to that which the masses pass by. In this way he promotes the natural development of all things without venturing to interfere.

Comment

"Think not," said the Lord Jesus, "that I came to destroy the law or the prophets; I came not to destroy, but to fulfill." There is a natural development which cannot be disturbed without producing injurious reactions. Whoever, therefore, takes upon himself the office of a teacher assumes a responsibility which is heavy. The words of the Lord to Peter are, when rightly comprehended, awful enough to warn off all but the most Spirit-pressed from attempting to preach to their fellowmen. "I will give unto thee the keys of the kingdom of heaven, and whatsoever thou shalt bind on earth shall be bound in heaven, and whatsoever thou shalt loose on earth shall be loosed in heaven." We dare not refuse our aid and guidance, but it requires omniscience to offer it as it ought to be given. By practicing non-action the wise man promotes development without marring it with the impress of his own personality.

Notes

(1) "Take time by the forelock." Remember that everything depends on being right in the beginning.

(2) "li"=1894 ft.

(3) I Pet. v, 8, 9.

(4) See chap. 29.

(5) I.e. if they ceased to "take thought for the morrow," and only cared to be true to themselves and their duty. Heb. iii, 14.

(6) "The common herd are full of incessant solicitude; the holy Man is simple and ignorant."—*Chuang-tzu.*

"Desire nothing to happen as you wish, but wish things to happen as they do."—*Epictetus.*

"Whatever is agreeable to thee, O Universe, is agreeable to me; nothing is early or late for me that is seasonable for you."—*Marcus Aurelius.*

"Desire is guided from without, will from within."—Annie Besant, *Ancient Wisdom.*

"One should neither rejoice at obtaining what is pleasant, nor sorrow in obtaining what is unpleasant."—*Bhagavad Gita.*

"One who has self-control, looks within at his mind, and in his mind there is no mind; he looks at his form, and in his form there is no form; he looks further and observes Nature, and in Nature there is no Nature."—*The Classic of Purity.*

(7) The student will here recall Cardinal Nicholas of Cusa (born near Treves A.D. 1401, died 1473) and his favorite phrase "learned ignorance," or "learned not-knowing." Wisdom is from within, it is born of the spirit; intellect is from without, it leads to superstition.

"If thou wilt know or learn anything profitably, desire to be unknown and to be little esteemed."—Thomas à Kempis.

CHAPTER 65

From the most ancient times those who have practiced the Tao have depended on the simplicity of the people rather than on their adroitness.

When the people are difficult to control it is because they possess too much worldly wisdom.

Who governs by worldly wisdom is a robber in the land; who governs without it is a blessing to the state.

To know these two axioms is to become a model. To understand how to be a model is indeed the mystery of energy.

Verily, deep and far-reaching is this mystery of energy. It is the opposite of all that is visible, but it leads to universal concord.

Comment

The Christ-man seeks nothing for himself; the worldly man ever cries "mine," rather than "my neighbor." The former is simple, the latter adroit. Wise indeed is that man who understands the "mystery of energy," the power of action which is desireless. Action which is desireless diverts no portion of its force toward bringing fruit to its author, hence, in the language of Paul, it is the foolish things and the weak things which confound the wise and the mighty. (*Vide* I. Cor. i, 27, 28). Because men fail to comprehend this, their best efforts, like Nebuchadnezzar's image, are part iron and part clay. No politician has yet risen to these sublime heights, no state has yet proven superior to the glamor of "worldly wisdom"; therefore, while seeking to cure the ills they know, they create fresh evils, the end of which they do not see. *Who governs by worldly wisdom is a robber in the land.*

CHAPTER 66

That which enables the rivers and the seas to become the rulers of all the water-courses is their ability to remain the lowest; it is on this account that they are the rulers of them all.[1] In like manner the Holy Man, if he wishes to direct the people must speak of himself as subject to them; if he wishes to lead them he must put himself in the background.[2] Hence the Sages are supreme, but the people are not burdened; they are in the vanguard, but the people are not harmed.[3] For this reason the whole Empire delights to exalt them, and no one feels annoyance.[4] Because they do not strive there is none who can strive with them.[5]

Comment

Disraeli's tribute to the Duke of Wellington provides an excellent illustration of the teaching in this chapter:

> "Thy calm mien
> Recalls old Rome, as much as thy high deed;
> Duty thine only idol, and serene
> When all are troubled; in the utmost need
> Prescient; thy country's servant ever seen,
> Yet sovereign of thyself whate'er may speed."
> —Quoted in Herbert Maxwell's *Life of Wellington*.

Notes

(1) The same illustration is used of the Tao in chap. 32.
(2) Comp. ch. 7.
It is man's wisdom which prevents him from being wise; it is his desire for lordship which keeps him from attaining power. The *post-mortem* fame of the Roman Emperor Aurelius rests on his lowliness rather than on his "dignities." The constitutional sovereignty of today safeguards the throne better than the sharpest tyranny of olden times.

"The secret of the Lord is with them that fear him."

Says Tung-kung-shu (B.C. 200), "When one places himself in his qualities below others, in character he is above them; when he places them behind those of others, in character he is before them."

Yang-hsiung (B.C. 53-A.D.) writes: "Men exalt him who humbles himself below them; and gives the precedence to him who puts himself behind them." (Quoted by Legge *loc cit.*)

(3) i. e. They do not rebel or disobey their superiors. Cf. chap. 60.

(4) Markgraf of Iyeyasu, who by means of the sword transformed old feudal Japan and laid the foundation of that country's greatness, when on his death bed sent for his grandson and said to him: "You will one day have to govern the Empire. Remember, the true way to govern the Empire is to have a mercy-loving and tender heart."

(5) See ch. 22.

CHAPTER 67

It was once generally affirmed that the greater the Self the more impossible it was to compare it with anything else.[1] Now it is just this greatness which makes it incomparable; should, however, a comparison be demanded, it would have to be described as the eternal, which is imperceptible. Now the Self has three treasures, to which it clings as to inseparables: the first is compassion,[2] the second, self-restraint, the third, nowhere venturing to claim precedence.

Compassionate—therefore irresistible![3]

Self-restrained—therefore enlarged!

Nowhere venturing to claim precedence—therefore efficient![4]

Nowadays men cast compassion on one side, yet expect to be irresistible! They discard self-restraint, yet look for enlargement; They forget to retire, yet demand precedence!—this is death.[5]

As regards compassion, rely on it when you would contend, and you will overcome; rely on it when you would protect, and you will succeed. Heaven is ever ready to deliver because of the protection compassion brings.[6]

Comment

"He shall not strive, nor cry aloud;
Neither shall anyone hear his voice in the streets.
A bruised reed shall he not break,
And smoking flax shall he not quench,
Till he send forth judgment unto victory,
And in his name shall the Gentiles hope."

(Matt. xii, 19-21.)

Notes

(1) True greatness cannot be included in any one class to the exclusion of the others, and therefore it cannot be classified.

(2) Maclagan, who translates *tz'u* as gentleness instead of compassion, notes that "Gentleness corresponds to the female element which appears more than once in the *Tao-teh-king*."

(3) Hsü-hui-hi notes that compassion is irresistible because it never exerts its strength until force is unavoidable.

(4) Lit. "a vessel of highest honor." Legge *loc cit.*

(5) Can the flower live when the root is gone?

(6) Students will observe that my translation differs materially from the renditions of previous laborers in the same field. Whether for better or for worse I must leave to the judgment of Chinese scholars, and the intuitions of those to whom the ancient philosopher is a teacher.

CHAPTER 68

The most skillful warriors are not warlike; the best fighters are not wrathful; the mightiest conquerors never strive; the greatest masters are ever lowly.

This is the glory of non-strife; and the might of utilization; these equal heaven, they were the goal of the ancients.

Comment

Desire for self-assertion is the controlling motive on the material plane—dogma contends with dogma, creed with creed, church with church. On the spiritual plane the sense of separateness which produces contention disappears and as the material is controlled by the moral, the physical by the spiritual, it follows that, centuries of contrary conceptions notwithstanding, the greatest might is that which does not contend. An anonymous writer has well said:

"Force and evil are no remedy. Use those means, and we shall find we only move the trouble from one quarter into another, and the difficulty we apparently get out of in one direction has come home to roost in another, stronger than ever. Goodness, and Goodness only, will destroy evil, and make our lives in this world—and in the next—smooth and comfortable."

CHAPTER 69

Military commanders have a saying:[1]

. I dare not act as host but only as a guest;[2] rather than advance an inch I would retire a foot.[3]

This marching without moving; bearing the invisible arm; regarding the enemy as if he were not; grasping the sword that is not.[4]

There is no calamity greater than making light of the enemy;[5] to make light of the enemy is to endanger my retention of the treasures.[6] Hence once the opposing forces have met it is the pitiful who conquer.[7]

Comment

"Jesus, therefore, perceiving that they were about to come and take him by force, to make him a king, withdrew again into the mountain himself alone," and was thereby endowed with a more powerful scepter than if he had accepted a visible crown. Refusing to play the part of a host or master, he gained the kingdom and became its lord.

Missionaries, and all who disturb the natural development of national moral culture, tearing down and destroying where they should only build and conserve, are acting as hosts in lands where they are uninvited guests. The chapter is a warning that it is only those who feel the pity of physical and moral force; who understand the danger that is inseparable from all attempts to present truth to the hostile, who ultimately win in the contest.

Notes

(1) The text does not say, as nearly every translator has translated it as, "A certain commander said so and so," but "The general policy of all great generals is thus and thus."

(2) I.e. I do not dare to act on my own initiative; before committing myself I wait to discover the intentions of the enemy. The "enemy" is in the text spoken of as the "host."

(3) The idea is that the holder of the Tao should always be more ready to yield than to give battle.

(4) Although inert he is ever on the alert, and ready for every emergency. Cf. I Pet. v. 8.

(5) A warning against allowing active passivity to become careless indifference. Cf. Eph. vi. 13-18.

(6) Vide. chap. 67. A determination to destroy the enemy regardless of the necessity for the act is contrary to compassion; it reveals an absence of self-restraint.

(7) Angry passions and impatient desires to join the battle are naturally aroused when the opposing forces are lying face to face, but here, as always, it is those who feel the pity of it all, but who are yet prepared for every eventuality, who win the day; their very sorrow that a battle is unavoidable, prevents their being hurried by the impetuosity of passion into some foolish and fatal move.

There is a story told of Admiral Dewey which aptly illustrates the military spirit which Lao-tzu is commending. The American ships were making magnificent target practice in Manila Bay, and the Spanish fleet was sinking. The Americans began to cheer. "Don't shout, boys," said Dewey. "The poor devils are dying."

CHAPTER 70

It is very easy to comprehend my teachings and to put them into practice. Yet there is no one in the world who is able either to comprehend, or to practice them.[1]

There is an originating principle for speech, an authoritative law for conduct,[2] but because this knowledge is lacking I am unknown.[3] Those who know Me are few; those who imitate Me are worthy. Hence the Holy Man wears coarse garments, but carries a jewel in his bosom.[4]

Comment

If a man be before his time, though he stand in the midst of the sun, he will appear to his contemporaries as one dwelling in darkness. The "Wisdom of God" has always been a mystery, and because the "Princes of this world" do not understand it they have in all ages "crucified the Lord of Glory." (I Cor. ii, 7, 8.)

Notes

(1) An analysis of the atmosphere is a different affair from its inhalation. There is a distinction between Truth and its expression. To intellectually comprehend the words in which Truth clothes herself, is not to grasp Truth herself. Truth can neither be written nor uttered. Truth is Spirit, and beside Truth there is nothing. Cf. John, vii, 17.

(2) Lit. "Words have an ancestor; affairs a ruler."

(3) Confucius, Lao-tzu's great contemporary, likewise complained that he was unknown. Cf. *Analects* xiv, 37.

(4) The chapter reminds us of the question of Jesus recorded in John viii, 43: "Why do ye not understand my speech? Even because ye cannot hear my word."

CHAPTER 71

The highest attainment is to know non-knowledge.[1] To regard ignorance as knowledge is a disease. Only by feeling the pain of this disease do we cease to be diseased. The perfected man, because he knows the pain of it, is free from this disease. It is for this reason that he does not have it.[2]

Comment

He who wills to do the Will, must know THAT which is beyond knowledge; he must ascend into the regions of the supersensuous. Listen to a few of the simpler sayings of the Master. "Resist not evil"; "Lay not up for yourselves treasures on earth"; "Take no thought . . . what ye shall eat or drink." Such sentences appeal to the heart but not to the head. They land us in the region where intellectual machinery is worth little more than old iron. Nevertheless, as Lao-tzu says, ignorance of this indicates disease, for Truth, whether a philosophy or a life, is:

> "The Somewhat which we name, but cannot know,
> Ev'n as we name a star, and only see
> His quenchless flashings forth, which ever show
> And ever hide him, and which are not he."

Notes

(1) "Non-knowledge in the sense of absolute knowledge. Everything that is absolute appears to us as nothing because all we know we know relatively."

(2) "To know what it is that you know, and to know what it is that you do not know—that is understanding."—Confucian *Analects,* ii. 17.

"If any man thinketh that he knoweth anything, he knoweth not yet as he ought to know."—Paul. (I Cor. viii, 2.)

CHAPTER 72

The limits of the greatest fear have been reached when the people cease to fear that which is to be feared.

Neither regard your lot as mean, nor despise the conditions of your birth, for that which is not despised arouses no disgust.

Hence although the Holy Man knows himself he makes no display; although he loves himself he seeks no reputation. On this account he rejects the one while clinging to the other.[1]

Comment

Discontent with the present and fear of the future constitute the inner life of the multitude, but those who have transcended the limitations of the seen, so that they neither enjoy nor fear the effects of sensation, have entered into a fear which is fearless. "Wherefore receiving a kingdom which cannot be shaken, let us have grace, whereby we may offer service well-pleasing to God with reverence and awe: for our God is a consuming fire." (Heb. xii, 28-29.)

Notes

(1) *Su-cheh* has the following: "The real self of man is as great as heaven and earth. Those who are ignorant of this look upon their physical frame as themselves, and are very careful to cherish that. Thus they know nothing excepting what they see and hear, and consequently are insignificant and rustic. Hence the instruction *'Do not regard your lot as mean!'* On the other hand there are those who knowing the greatness of their real selves, are vexed at the contracted limits into which they are born. They long to escape from them but cannot. They do not know that the more they chafe (at their surroundings) and hanker after something else, the more heavily their limitations press upon them. Hence the instruction *'Nor despise the condi-*

tions of your birth.' The Sage on the other hand is without regrets, and without dissatisfactions. He lives as one of the people; he is in harmony with the Tao. He knows no difference between the wide and the narrow, the clean and the dirty. Because he does not despise life he learns that life is not to be despised."

Cf. Paul's witness concerning himself "I have learned, in whatsoever state I am, therein to be content. I know how to be abased, and I know also how to abound: in everything and in all things I have learned the secret both to be filled and to be hungry, both to abound and to be in want. I can do all things in him that strengtheneth me." (Phil. iv, 11-12.)

CHAPTER 73

The recklessly rash die. The cautiously courageous live. Of these two courses it is uncertain which is advantageous and which is disadvantageous, for who can explain why heaven disapproves? Therefore even the Holy Man feels a difficulty here.[1] This is the way of heaven:

Goodwill, which surely overcomes.

Silence, which certainly responds.[2]

Without being summoned, spontaneously arriving.

Acting leisurely, but planning effectively.

Heaven's net spreads everywhere, wide in mesh, yet losing nothing.[3]

Comment

"Merry and bright are the waves today,
They dance round our boat like children at play;
But though wild winds should rise and dark waters roar,
Till our light bark be cast a wreck on the shore;
Still the strength which awes us is not found here,
But beneath where all is calm and clear;
Where feeling the weight of the law's behest,
In the depths of the ocean is calm and rest."

—Vantia Bailey

Notes

(1) The higher the knowledge, the greater the responsibility, the narrower the path.

(2) "Look at heaven there," answered Confucius, "does it speak? And yet the seasons run their appointed courses and all things in nature grow up in their time. Look at heaven there: does it speak?"—*Confucian Analects*.

(3)   "Though the mills of God grind slowly
        Yet they grind exceeding small.
    Though with patience he stands waiting,
        With exactness grinds he all."

—Friederich von Logau, Longfellow's translation.
"Und alles ist Frucht, und alles is Samen."—*Schiller*.

CHAPTER 74

Why use death as a deterrent, when the people have no fear of death?

Even supposing they shrank from death as from a monster, and by playing on their terror I could slay them, should I dare?[1]

There is one who inflicts sentence of death. To usurp his functions and to kill would be to assume the role of the Master-Carpenter. There are few who can act as Master-Carpenter without cutting their hands.[2]

Comment

Dr. Franz Hartmann, of Leipzig, comments as follows on this chapter in the *Lotusblüthen*: "The death penalty as a deterrent measure is a legacy from an ignorant generation. That which incites men to action cannot be killed. The evil inclination toward crime when driven from the body by execution is only thereby made still more generally harmful, because it again influences others, and leads them to perform similar deeds to those for which the execution took place. Moreover, through suffering the wrong of execution, desires for retaliation are aroused in the soul of the executed, and in this way he is made more dangerous than before. What is the use of destroying the tool, while the ringleader is beyond reach? It will be easy for him to find another instrument. What is the use of banishing the evil from the house, when it can readily find another dwelling? Better endeavor to reform the criminal, by bringing him to a better conception of things, and in this way transform the evil into a good spirit."

Notes

(1) Thos. Kingsmill's translation is illuminative: "With folk who have no fear of death, what object is there in making its apprehension a deterrent? How should we dare

to apprehend and to execute people who dread death as the greatest terror?"

(2) Cf. chap. 30.

Cf. a saying by Confucius; he is expounding the fundamental principle of all Chinese law, the veneration of the inferior for the superior, an idea which has strong affinities with the philosophy of the ancient Greeks. "Why when governing, depend on capital punishment? Seek righteousness and the people will be righteous. The relation between the rulers and the ruled is like that between the wind and the grass. The grass must bend when the wind blows across it." Confucian *Analects*, xii. 19.

CHAPTER 75

The people suffer from famine because of the multitude of taxes consumed by their superiors. Because of this they suffer from famine. The people are difficult to govern because of the officiousness of their superiors; because of this they are difficult to govern. Men are continually[1] dying because they lust after life; because of this they frequently die.

It is only those with whom life is no object who truly value life.[2]

Comment

A warning to rulers and to ruled—The only safety of either a state or an individual is to seek first the kingdom of God and its righteousness. The more is grasped the less is possessed.

Notes

(1) Literally "readily," "easily," "without difficulty."
(2) Cf. chaps. 53, 65.
Huai-nan-tzu (B.C. 179) illustrates this chapter with a story: "Tzu-fei of the kingdom of King (the present provinces of Hunan and Hupeh) went to a certain place to obtain a very valuable two-edged sword. As he was returning with his prize a terrible storm overtook the vessel, and two scaly dragons wrapped themselves round the ship. Going to the captain Tzu-fei said, 'If this continues how can we live?' The captain confessed that it was the first time he had encountered such an experience, whereupon Tzu-fei bracing himself for a conflict, bared his arm and pulling his two-edged weapon from its sheath said, 'One may discuss benevolence, righteousness and honor with heroes, but to waylay or capture them is impossible. Here, in the midst of this sea I am but a mass of rotten flesh and crumbling

bones, though I lose my sword what matters it? Is there anything at all to which I cling?' Leaping into the waters he thrust the dragons through and cut off their heads. He thus saved the lives of all his fellow passengers, and stilled the storm, and for this was subsequently suitably rewarded by his prince."

CHAPTER 76

At birth man is supple and weak, at death rigid and strong. So with inanimate nature—say the vegetable creation—in its early growth it is pliable and brittle, at death it is decayed and withered. It follows that rigidity and strength are the way to death; pliability and gentleness the way to life.

Hence a soldier who is arrogant cannot conquer; the tree which is strong is doomed.[1]

The firm and the great occupy the lower place, the pliable and the meek[2] the higher.

Comment

"Man has a thousand purposes. Death comes one morning and ten thousand wait." "Man has a thousand, a myriad plans for himself; God has only one plan for him." In these Chinese proverbs we find the aroma of the present chapter. Translated into the more prosaic language of the West we express the root idea of Lao-tzu's aphorisms thus: Whatever makes for the increase of self leads to death; Life is found only when self yields to the Self. "Wherefore the Scripture saith, God resisteth the proud, but giveth grace to the humble. Be subject therefore unto God." (James iv, 6-7.)

Notes

(1) Having become fit to be used as timber it is in danger from the woodman's axe. The wood rendered "doomed" is literally "altogether." Dr. Carus compares it to the German *alle*, "it is gone," "finished," or "doomed." No literal rendering of the Chinese is possible. Cf. *Taoist Texts* by Balfour, p. 83.

(2) The phrases "supple and weak," "pliability and gentleness," "pliable and meek" are represented in Chinese by the same hieroglyphs—an illustration of the difficulties and dangers which threaten the European who attempts to render Lao-tzu into intelligible and easy English.

CHAPTER 77

The Divine Way is like the drawing of a bow, it brings down the high and exalts the low.[1] Where there is superfluity it takes away, where there is deficiency it imparts. It is the way of heaven to diminish abundance, and supplement deficiency.[2]

The way of man is not so. He depletes the deficient, that he may supplement the superfluous.

Who is able to have a superabundance for the service of the world? Only the possessor of the Tao! Hence the Holy Man acts without priding himself on his actions, completes his work without lingering on it; he has no desire to display his superiority.[3]

Comment

Man grasps all; God gives all. Man makes himself great; God is content to be small. Man loves to surpass others; God strives that all may be one. A Chinese commentator suggests that Heaven, because universal, equalizes, but that man, because exceedingly parochial, differentiates.

Notes

(1) So Prof. Giles renders this sentence in his *Remains of Lao-Tzu;* he adds an explanatory note: "When the bow held vertically (as the Chinese hold it) is drawn, the upper nock is brought down while the lower nock is brought up."

(2) Dr. Carus remarks on this passage that "while the first sentence is almost literally like Christ's doctrine, 'whosoever shall exalt himself shall be abased,' the second sentence is the reverse of the New Testament teaching that, 'Whosoever hath, to him shall be given, and he shall have abundance; but whosoever hath not, from him shall be taken away even that which he hath.' (Matt. xiii, 12.)" The difference is, however, only verbal. Christ and Lao-tzu both teach that the Divine Way is equality, equilibrium,

and that whatever contravenes this is wrong. Cf. Luke, iii, 4-6.

(3) Cf. chap. 2. Says Huai-nan-tzu: "He does not depend on the respect of others for his power, nor upon possession for his wealth, nor upon brute force for his strength; but it able to soar between the firmament above and the waters below, in company with his creator."—*Taoist Texts* by Balfour, p. 92.

"The divine Way," "The Way of Heaven" is in the Chinese "The Tao of Heaven." So also "The Way of man" in the text is in the original "The Tao of Man."

CHAPTER 78

Nothing is so flexible as water, yet for attacking that which is hard nothing surpasses it. There is nothing which supplants it.

The weak overcome the strong, the soft control the hard. Everyone knows this, but no one practices it.[1]

Hence a Sage has said—"Who bears his country's reproach is hailed as the lord of his nation's altars. Who bears his country's misfortunes is called the Empire's chief."

Truth, when expressed in speech, appears paradoxical.[2]

Comment

Said St. Paul: "When I am weak then am I strong." "For we also are weak with him, but we shall live with him by the power of God toward you."

"Measure thy love by loss instead of gain;
  Not by the wine drunk, but by the wine poured forth,
  For love's strength standeth in love's sacrifice,
  And whoso suffers most hath most to give."

Notes

(1) "The Tongue is an instrument yielding and pliant
    Yet safe in the mouth, it ever remains,
    While the teeth are inflexible, hard and defiant,
    And frequently broken to pay for their pains."
      —*Chinese Ode,* quoted by Arthur Smith in his *Chinese Proverbs.*

(2) This sentence more properly belongs to the next chapter. Cf. chap. 70.

CHAPTER 79

To compromise a great hate leaves ill-will behind; that only is a blessing which produces tranquillity.

Therefore the Holy Man does not pry into other people's affairs,[1] even when he holds the left-hand bond,[2] possessing the attributes of the Tao, he quietly holds his own; he who lacks the qualities of Tao strives to put everybody right.[3]

It is heaven's way to be without favorites,[4] and to be always on the side of the good man.[5]

Comment

The wise man is more concerned with the steadiness and direction of his own thoughts than with the actions of others. By his care to be himself unsullied to the very innermost recesses of his being, he purifies the atmosphere wherever he goes, and accomplishes more than he could were he ever reproaching what he considers untimely. Therefore the cry of the Hebrew prophet, "Be ye clean ye that bear the vessels of the Lord." (Isa. lii, 11.)

Notes

(1) In colloquial Chinese he does not blow aside the fur, to see if it contains burs or chips.

(2) "Contracts were written on two bamboo slips which fitted together, the left one containing the debit or obligations, the right one containing the credits or dues."—Carus, *loc cit.*

The Sage is content with having the truth himself, without seeking to impose his knowledge on everybody else.

(3) Cf. Matt. vii, 1-5, vide *Tao-Teh-King* chap. 60.

(4) Cf. Rom. viii, 28.

(5) Literally—"The Heavenly Tao is without relatives; it ever sides with the good man."

CHAPTER 80

A state may be small, and the population sparse, yet the people should be taught not to rely on force; they should be made to comprehend the gravity of death, and the futility of emigration. Then, though they had boats and carts, they would have no use for them; though they had armor and weapons they would not display them. They should be taught to return to the use of the quippo; to be content with their food, their clothing, their dwellings, and to be happy in their traditions. Though neighboring states were within sight, and the people should hear the barking of their dogs and the crowing of their cocks, they would grow old and die without visiting them.[1]

Comment

Better be a hermit, minus the comforts of civilization, than a millionaire chained to many earthly possessions. Montaigne nobly says, "Let us betimes bid our company farewell . . . We should reserve a storehouse for ourselves, and wholly free, wherein we may hoard up and establish our true liberty and principal retreat and solitariness." "Jesus said unto him, If thou wouldst be perfect, go sell that thou hast, and give to the poor, and thou shalt have treasure in heaven; and come follow me." "A man's life consisteth not in the abundance of things which he possesseth."

Notes

(1) *Su-cheh* sums up the chapter in a sentence: "If the inner brings satisfaction, the outer will have no attractions."

A Chinese paper laments the degeneracy of present times in the following language: "In ancient times men lived in caves and holes of the earth. They wore leaves for clothing.

They used earthenware of the rudest description, their carts had no tires, to record events they simply knotted a cord. In ancient times sovereign and people all sat on mats on the floor. In ancient times the sovereign invited some one to take his place while he retired. The feudal system prevailed. Now every one of these customs is obsolete, and we all know what we have at the present day."—*Su Pao.*

The Bhagavatam says: "While there is the bare ground, why labor for beds? While there is your own arm, why labor for a pillow? While the palms of your hands may be joined, why trouble yourself for dishes and platters? While there are barks on trees, why labor for raiment?"—*Dialogues on The Hindu Philosophy* by Rev. K. M. Banerjca.

CHAPTER 81

Sincere words are not (necessarily) pleasant, nor are pleasant words (necessarily) sincere.

The good are not (necessarily) skillful debaters, nor are skillful debaters (necessarily) good men.[1]

The wise are not (necessarily) well informed, nor are the well informed (necessarily) wise.[2]

The Holy Man does not accumulate. He works for others, yet ever has abundance for himself; he gives to others, yet himself ever possesses superabundance.

The divine way is advantageous, without danger; the way of the Sages is effective without struggle.[3]

Comment

The book closes as it began. In the first chapter we saw the Tao differentiate and lose itself that the universe might become, and in the last our attention is directed to the Man in whom the Tao is incarnate—ever active, but keeping nothing for himself.

"A man there was, though some did count him mad,
The more he gave away, the more he had."[4]

Notes

(1) Confucius remarked, "With plausible speech and fine manners will seldom be found moral character."—*Analects*.

(2) Confucius remarked, "A man who possesses moral worth will always have something to say worth listening to; but a man who has something to say is not necessarily a man of moral worth."—*Analects*.

(3) The last sentence is according to the rendering of T. W. Kingsmill.

Literally—"Heaven's Tao benefits but injures not; the Holy Man's Tao acts but strives not."

(4) Quoted by Legge from Bunyan, *loc. cit.*